"This book is the monk's lectio of a lifetime. As prior he knows of what he reports: we imitate Christ Jesus by washing feet. In return we know the God who gives us birth."

—Meg Funk, OSB, Our Lady of Grace Monastery, Beech Grove, Indiana

"No one has taught me more about faith, calm, and clarity in the service of humanity than Cyprian Consiglio. What a grace it is to have his open-hearted wisdom and his unswayable spirit in the world, teaching us how to live for something larger than self and deeper than dogma."

—Pico Iyer, author of *The Art of Stillness*

"After decades in a contemplative hermitage, Cyprian Consiglio has come to know God as intimate, infinite love, available to anyone willing to take Christ's path of self-emptying. At a time when too many Christians cling to the image of God as a thunderbolt-flinging Zeus or devote themselves to lesser gods entirely—money, military might, political power—Consiglio offers a joyful, compelling vision of what is possible when human beings encounter divine reality. *The God Who Gave You Birth* is a marvelous and potentially life-changing book."

—Paula Huston, author of *One Ordinary Sunday: A Meditation on the Mystery of the Mass*

"*The God Who Gave You Birth* offers a timely, accessible, and delightful reflection on the theology of *kenosis*—the self-emptying of God in the incarnation, which the church is called to emulate like yeast that 'acts by disappearing' and salt that 'acts by dissolving.' It is a gifted teacher who can explore complex theological concepts in refreshing and accessible ways, and Fr. Cyprian has done just that. His book gently but unapologetically explores the Christian mystical tradition on its own terms, not in isolation from other contemplative traditions, but in a way that celebrates Christianity's distinctive contributions. His creative use of Scripture, hymnody, psychology, and Christian symbolism are gently woven together to create a sustained exploration on the meaning of kenosis for the modern contemplative."

> —Fr. Vincent Pizzuto, PhD, University of San Francisco, and author of *Contemplating Christ: The Gospels and the Interior Life*

The God Who Gave You Birth

A Spirituality of Kenosis

Cyprian Consiglio, OSB Cam

LITURGICAL PRESS
Collegeville, Minnesota

www.litpress.org

1   2   3   4   5   6   7   8   9

Library of Congress Cataloging-in-Publication Data

Names: Consiglio, Cyprian, author.
Title: The God who gave you birth : a spirituality of kenosis / Cyprian Consiglio, OSB Cam.
Description: Collegeville, Minnesota : Liturgical Press, [2021] | Includes bibliographical references. | Summary: "Through Scripture, the thoughts of theologians, Benedictine monasticism, Jewish and Islamic traditions, along with his own personal reflections, Cyprian Consiglio, OSB Cam, explores how we think of God as Jesus reveals God to be"—Provided by publisher.
Identifiers: LCCN 2021004723 (print) | LCCN 2021004724 (ebook) | ISBN 9780814666579 (paperback) | ISBN 9780814666586 (epub) | ISBN 9780814666586 (mobi) | ISBN 9780814666586 (pdf)
Subjects: LCSH: Incarnation.
Classification: LCC BT220 .C66 2021 (print) | LCC BT220 (ebook) | DDC 232/.1—dc23
LC record available at https://lccn.loc.gov/2021004723
LC ebook record available at https://lccn.loc.gov/2021004724

To my Camaldolese sisters and brothers,
monks and oblates, and especially the monks of
New Camaldoli who honored me with
being their servant

You were unmindful of the Rock that bore you;
you forgot the God who gave you birth.
Deuteronomy 32:18

Zeus and the priests of Baal

Although you are sovereign in strength, you judge
   with mildness,
and with forbearance you govern us;
for you have power to act whenever you choose.[1]

One day some years ago I was leafing through a wonderful children's book, D'Aulaires' *Book of Greek Myths*, which I loved as a child. Although well into my adult years, I enjoyed reading it again, remembering how captivated I was by all these myths when I was a kid. But when I got to the page about Zeus, as I looked at the colored drawing of this greatest of the gods, it suddenly occurred to me that so many Christians talk about God not as Jesus introduces God to us, but more as if God were Zeus! The image of Zeus in the book could have been one of the images of God the Father that I have seen on great church ceilings and in illustrated Bibles, sitting on top of a mountain, irritated, jealous, and a little capricious, shooting down lightning bolts and causing earthquakes just so we remember how awesome He is.

Some of the ideas about God that we get from the Jewish Scriptures could play into this mentality, if we take the

1. Wis 12:18.

stories literally. For example, there is the graphic story in the First Book of Kings about Elijah having a contest with the priests of the Canaanite god Baal to see if their god or the God of Israel would be the one to accept a sacrificial bull.[2] The priests of Baal go at it first, and they call on the name of Baal from morning until noon, until they were worn out, limping around the altar that they had made. All the while Elijah is taunting them, saying, "Cry aloud! Surely he is a god; either he is meditating, or he has wandered away, or he is on a journey, or perhaps he is asleep and must be awakened." The pagan priests then cut themselves with swords and lances until blood is gushing from their wounds, and they rave on and on but, alas, no response.

Then it's Elijah's turn. He surrounds the sacrificial bull with trenches and piles up wood around it, and then fills the trenches with water and pours water over the wood too, just to make it as impossible as could be. Yet when he calls on the name of the Lord, fire falls and consumes the burnt offering, the wood, the stones, and the dust—and even licks up the water in the trench!

This story would be comical if it didn't end so gruesomely; at that point Elijah has the people seize the priests of Baal, and he slaughters them in the Wadi Kishon.

2. 1 Kgs 18:20-39

Our ideas about God and religion tend to match the stage of our own maturity and the level of our own consciousness. Developmental psychology tells us that we human beings begin life with a magical view of the universe, and so we also have a magical view of God and religion. (God is the Wizard of Oz and I am Harry Potter.) Then we tend to move into a more mythical way of thinking, followed by what developmental psychology calls rational, pluralistic, and integral views of reality, and so rational, pluralistic, and integral views of God and religion. This can apply both to individuals as well as to entire cultures.

We need to keep in mind that a story like the one above from the Book of Kings comes from the obscure magical-mythical age of the Jewish tradition, sometimes with just the slightest thread of connection to history. One of the most fascinating things about this era is the understanding of God and "the gods"—capital "G" God as opposed to small "g" gods. According to the mentality of that time there *were* all kinds of gods with a small "g," and often the stories we hear from that era are about whose small "g" god is bigger and stronger. So here in the Book of Kings we have a battle between the (small "g") god Baal and (capital "G") God who is, in a sense, the (small "g") god of Israel.

It's a battle of the gods!

You see, we monotheists don't necessarily deny that there are other gods, in the broadest sense of what a god is. A god is any supra-human being or power that we worship. A "god" in this sense could even be fame or power. A "god" in this sense could be wealth, for instance, which is nearly personified in the gospels as the greedy demon *mammon*. Remember St. Paul too exhorts his readers to put to death, among other things, greed, which he says *is idolatry*.[3] "You shall have no other (small "g") god before me," says God (capital "G"). In other words: do not worship *anything* but me. We agree with the prophet Muhammad about that, at least: *la-illah ha il-Allah*—"There is no god but God"; there is no *lah* but *Al-lah*—God. The only real Divine One is God, the one who Abraham met. In Islam Muhammad thought he was calling people back to the revelation of Abraham. And when he conquered Mecca he destroyed all the images of the deities that were in the Kabbah (every one, that is, except for a fresco of Abraham and a painting of Jesus and Mary, interestingly enough).

So many of our world government and economic leaders, even those who profess some form of monotheistic religion, obviously worship other gods—the power of the economy, military strength, fame—and even use, or misuse, the name of God or credit God with whatever is gained. This is a perennial tendency. It seems as if even when Constantine decided to decriminalize Christianity in the fourth century, it was because he thought that the (small "g") god of Christianity had helped him win a battle, rather than the Roman gods. Catholic mentality hadn't changed much by the six-

3. Col 3:5.

teenth century, when the church credited Our Lady of the Rosary with helping the so-called Holy League win a battle against the Ottoman Turks at Lepanto in southwestern Greece.

It's a very primitive mindset, one that has not yet caught up with the revelation of Jesus, who didn't win military victories or start trade wars or bully his way into anything, but showed only the power of sacrificial love, crucified love, emptiness. We have to be careful when we hear stories like these to not take them as an exhortation to fall back into that magical-mythical and pre-Christian mindset, as if we were talking about a small "g" god who is going to give victory to our football team over someone else's team, or who we hope is going to give us luck in the stock market.

Instead, we need to think of God as Jesus introduces God to us.

We Christians might be tempted to blame this magical-mythical view of God on the so-called "Old Testament," the Jewish Scriptures, and the image of God we catch there. Yet there are a variety of images of God offered in the books of the Jewish Scriptures as the people of the first covenant themselves grew in their understanding of who God is. In the Book of Wisdom, from a much later era than the Book of Kings, already there is a pretty evolved idea of who and how God is. Although sovereign in strength, God judges with mildness and governs with forbearance because God has power to act whenever God chooses. That calls to mind one of the best pieces of advice I ever received about leadership.

It was this: "When you have real authority you don't need to grab for power." That's God. God has real authority and so doesn't need to jealously *grab* for power nor make sure that we human beings always feel like powerless little peons, as Zeus and the other gods are always doing to mortals.

The late, great Catholic novelist Flannery O'Connor described her age in this way: it is " 'an unbelieving age but one that is markedly and lopsidedly spiritual,' at once 'an age of searchers and discoverers,' and 'an age that has domesticated despair and learned to live with it happily.' " And it has a "kind of sub-religion which expresses its ultimate concern in images that have not yet broken through to show any recognition of a God who has revealed himself."[i]

If that was true in the mid-twentieth century, how much truer is it now in the twenty-first? Our job is to show the world God as Jesus reveals God to be.

this is what God is like

There is a marvelous exchange between the apostle Philip and Jesus in the Gospel of John. Philip says to Jesus, "Lord, show us the Father, and we will be satisfied." And I love Jesus' reply to him. Jesus said, "Have I been with you all this time, Philip, and you still do not know me? Whoever has seen me has seen the Father!"[4] You want to know what God

---

4. John 14:8-9.

is like? Jesus says. I'm what God is like! If you've seen me you've seen God! This is what God is like and this is what God does: God travels light, God is merciful, God forgives and reconciles, God heals, God brings people to an understanding of their own dignity, God overturns the wisdom of this world, the wisdom of expediency and usefulness and power and authority, and instead rules with love, with mercy, from within and from behind, through service and what looks like weakness—the very opposite of what all the success seminars teach us. God is someone who washes your feet. God is not afraid to be broken up and crushed like wheat and grapes and passed out as a meal to be consumed. God is crucified love, unconditional acceptance. As our Muslim sisters and brothers say, God is *ir-Rahman ir-Rahim*—All-Merciful, All-Compassionate. As our Jewish forbears would say, God is a veritable womb of mercy.

That's what Jesus was like; that's what God is like.

Saint Paul's definitions of Jesus are the ones I rely on the most if I need to succinctly explain who we believe Jesus to be, even though they are sometimes more like riddles or Zen-like *koans* than formulas: "He is the image [*ikon*] of the invisible God," Paul writes in the Letter to the Colossians, and "in him the fullness of God was pleased to dwell."[5] This is an amazing assertion, that this is what God is like, wrapped up in a Palestinian Jewish man who walked dusty

5. Col 1:15, 19.

roads and ate and drank with other human beings. And this is our justification for gazing at the image of Jesus—"If you've seen me you've seen the Father!" It's the reason we spend so much time mulling over the Scriptures, especially the gospels, to catch a better glimpse. There's an old piece of wisdom that says we become what we gaze at, and that's why we mull over the Scriptures too, not just to figure out Jesus, but to figure out who we are, to become what he was so as to do what he did, and even greater things, to carry on the work of the reign of God. As Jesus was the image, so our tradition tells us that we are the "image of the image." And Jesus' beloved disciple John tells us clearly that "we will be like him, for we will see him as he is."[6]

Jesus shows us that the very nature of God is unconditional compassion toward the human world. The very nature of God, as the liturgist Nathan Mitchell wrote, is "love without an opposite," unimpeachable love for creatures and creation. God is the One who cherishes people and makes them free. God's *will* is always and only a willing of good. God's *power* is always and only a power exercised on behalf of those who need it—the poor, the outcast, the despised, the marginalized, the wretched and lonely, the abandoned. We have to view everything else from the optic of the ultimate revelation of God in Jesus, who shows us that God is

6. 1 John 3:2.

neither angry nor vengeful—precisely because God has no "ego" to defend like the gods on Mount Olympus do.[ii]

That's what ought to come to mind when we read these words in the Book of Wisdom: "Although you are sovereign in strength, you judge with mildness, and with great forbearance you govern us; for you have power to act whenever you choose."[7] Or as Psalm 86 sings, "For you, O Lord, are good and forgiving, / abounding in steadfast love to all who call on you."[8] That's the good news.

to act by disappearing

There are two parables in the Gospel of Matthew that Jesus uses to give two very important images of the reign of God.

First of all he says that the reign of God is like a mustard seed that someone took and sowed in a field, "the smallest of all the seeds, but when it has grown it is the greatest of shrubs." And the reign of God, he says, is "like yeast that a woman took and mixed in with three measures of flour until all of it was leavened."[9] Hans Urs von Balthsar wrote that this is how the church "seeks its mission in the profane world that surrounds it: to be yeast that acts while disappearing."[iii] As a matter of fact both of these images, the seed and the yeast, act by disappearing, by dissolving, by

7. Wis 12:18.
8. Ps 86:5.
9. Matt 13:31-33.

dying. What a strange and powerful image for an individual, a community, the church—to act by disappearing.

Von Balthasar is writing here about why the church would go "beyond its confines" toward its separated Christian brothers and sisters, as well as to the Jewish people and non-Christians, explaining that this is "the movement of a self-emptying of God and Christ," so that it could be what he calls a "disinterested church," meaning a church that doesn't seek its own glory, but the glory of its Lord and union as love. To be like a seed that falls into the ground and dies, to be like yeast in the dough, to act by dissolving and disappearing. And yet, as Jesus also says about the seed in the Gospel of John, if that seed dies "it bears much fruit."[10]

This is what it means to be church, to be a follower of Jesus, to be like God: to imitate the self-emptying of God and Christ.

And so it is for us. We are supposed to be like yeast, too, like a seed that dies. We could add one more image that Matthew recounts Jesus saying: we are supposed to be like salt, the "salt of the earth,"[11] yet another element that acts by disappearing and dissolving. But in that dissolving, in dying, in a sense, the earth gets flavored, the dough is raised, a great bush rises up. The "profane world" that surrounds us, in which we are immersed, gets lifted up *by our very presence*, even if that presence be a silent hidden one. Saint

10. John 12:24.
11. Matt 5:13.

Thérèse of Lisieux, from her hidden life in the Carmelite monastery, described it this way: "In the heart of the Church, my mother, I will be love, and thus I will be all things,"[iv] like yeast in the dough, like salt in the earth, like a seed that dies.

One other use of this image of the seed or the yeast: we could think of our humanity, too, even our very bodies, as the field or as the dough. And God has planted a seed in that field too; God has put yeast into the dough of our being—the Holy Spirit, who, as Paul wrote in the Letter to the Romans, is "poured into our hearts,"[12] into the very center of our being, and brings the whole of our being to its glory from the inside out. Rather than being like Zeus— jealous and angry, tossing lightning bolts down from the sky—I think God is more like yeast, who in some way dissolves inside us as the Spirit so that we might share in the divine nature.

The influential Spanish Indian theologian Raimundo Panikkar wrote about this dissolving and disappearing in regard to the Eucharist. Before turning to theology, his first degree was in chemistry. He uses a verb that describes a chemical process—"volatilize," which means to evaporate or disperse like a vapor—as a metaphor for what God does for us, in us, as Eucharist. If we take the sacramental language of this most fundamental Christian rite literally, in

12. Rom 5:5.

consuming the consecrated host and wine we claim to be "eating God." We receive and swallow God definitively, Panikkar says, and what follows then is a sublimation of God's own self, "according to the chemical connotation of such a concept." And God volatilizes, "changes into a gaseous state of function, of horizon, of ideal, of mystical dimension."[v]

This is God's own *kenosis*. God becomes something in us.

Christ consciousness

The phrase "Christ consciousness" has worked its way into modern vocabulary, similar to the idea of "the universal Christ." This is no doubt due to Christianity's rubbing elbows with contemporary spiritual movements that show a keen interest for contemplative practice, particularly as taught by the Asian traditions with their practical disciplines such as yoga, and various forms of meditation with roots in Buddhism. I am somewhat hesitant about the phrase, not because it is not a valid concept but, first of all, because I am afraid that it is sometimes used to force Christianity to make sense in Buddhist or Hindu terms, while in the mean time dismissing some of Christianity's core tenets. Secondly, I'm afraid that some folks dismiss the vocabulary of Christian mystics as somehow less enlightened because Christian mystics do not articulate their experience in the same way that some Asian mystics do. Someone told me once, for instance, that if St. Teresa of Avila had been as enlightened as Shankara, the eighth-century Indian mystic and philosopher of non-duality, she would have expressed her experience in the same way that he did. This seems to needlessly dismiss the great Spanish saint's own experience. But perhaps even more practically, I am hesitant about this phrase because one could get the impression that "Christ consciousness" is something that can be achieved by just the right technique, the right posture, or the right words in the right language.

At the same time, I agree that there *is* such a thing as Christ consciousness. Saint Paul explains what it is very clearly in the great hymn contained in the Letter to the Philippians, which in the Roman liturgical tradition we sing every Saturday at evening prayer. It's known as the "kenosis hymn." "Let the same mind be in you that was in Christ Jesus," Paul says, "who,

> though he was in the form of God,
>> did not regard equality with God
>> as something to be exploited,
> but emptied himself,
>> taking the form of a slave,
>> being born in human likeness.
> And being found in human form,
>> he humbled himself
>> and became obedient to the point of death—
>> even death on a cross."[13]

13. Phil 2:5-8.

The key word here, of course, is the Greek word *kenosis*, the act of self-emptying, which will be our ongoing theme.

The other interesting Greek verb in that passage is *harpagmos*. There are various translations of it—Christ Jesus did not deem equality with God something to be "exploited," something to be "clung to" or "treasured jealously" or even "robbed." My favorite translation of this word, used in both the New American and New Jerusalem Bibles, is "grasped at." Christ Jesus did not deem equality with God, divinity, something to be grasped at. Rather, he emptied himself.

And this is how we too realize Christ consciousness, the same way Christ Jesus did, not by exploiting, robbing, or grasping at divinity by some technique or manipulation, but by self-emptying, or emptying our self.

But while we are on the topic of Christ consciousness and the universal Christ, here we bump into another slippery slope. There may be a tendency to separate Christ from Jesus. Orthodox Christianity would never completely separate the title "Christ" from the person of Jesus, even though it would carefully *distinguish* Christ from Jesus. And this is important in a way that may not seem obvious at first, specifically in regard to kenosis.

We might think of this kenosis mainly as the self-emptying of Jesus, who renounces his will for the Father's, even to the point of death on the cross. But the Letter to the Hebrews tells us that when Christ came into the world, he said, "See, God, I have come to do your will, O God."[14] That's the kenosis of *Christ*. The male human being Jesus was not at the right hand of the Father from all eternity. It is the Word, the Second Person of the Trinity, who was always with God and who was God, who we call the Christ, who became flesh and was named Jesus.

There is a little prayer in the Roman Rite of the Mass that is considered one of the "secret prayers," one of the prayers that the presider can say *sotto voce*, not necessarily proclaimed to the whole assembly, that is actually one of the most beautiful prayers in the liturgy. It is also one of the few places where the Roman Church speaks boldly about our participation in divinity (although *sotto voce*!). While pouring a drop of water into the wine the priest says, "By the mystery of this water and wine, / may we come to share in the divinity of Christ / who humbled himself to share in our humanity." Every now and then a priest will change the wording and instead say that we "come to share the divinity of *Jesus* who came to share in our humanity." The problem is, yes, we can share the divinity of Jesus, but it isn't Jesus who came to share our humanity. *Christ* did, when the Word, the Second Person of the Trinity, became flesh, became Jesus.

14. Heb 10:7.

We are back to mythological images again, and we might imagine a fully formed male named Jesus sitting at the right hand of an older male (the Father) who looks just like Jesus, only older, with a white beard instead of a dark one. And that Jesus, the son, gets sent "down" to earth from heaven in the form of a baby boy. There is a phrase from the Book of Wisdom that the Church uses at Christmas to describe the incarnation: "your all-powerful Word leaped from heaven, from the royal throne."[15] This is not the human, male Jesus who "leaps down" from heaven like a god descending from Mount Olympus; it's the Word, God the Word who becomes flesh. We do not claim that the human Jesus existed from all eternity. The Second Person of the Trinity, even before Jesus was born, was the Word, and it is that Word-made-flesh in Jesus that we call the Christ.

Why this is significant and why I'm making such a big deal about it in terms of this kenosis is because this means that it is *God's own self* (in the Second Person of the Trinity) who does not deem divinity something to be grasped at! This is God (in the Second Person of the Trinity) relinquishing a place in "some heaven light years away" or on Mount Olympus. This is God not clinging to holiness as separateness but instead choosing to be *Emmanuel*—God-With-Us, God the Word who is not squeamish about being bound in our *carne*.

15. Wis 18:15.

The incarnation is the kenosis of God, the self-emptying of God in order to be human. As the poet Christian Wiman wrote, kenosis "refers to the kind of self-emptying that God" *in Jesus* "performed in both the incarnation and the crucifixion."[vi] While the crucifixion, as well as his whole life of selfless service, is Christ Jesus' kenosis, the incarnation is Christ-God the Word's self-emptying to become the human Jesus.

Commenting on this same kenosis hymn, Pope Benedict wrote that the words of this hymn mark a decisive turning point in the history of mysticism and point out what is sparkling and new in the message of Jesus: "God descends, to the point of death on the Cross" and we "ascend to God by accompanying God on this descending path."[vii]

God descends. And we ascend by imitating God—by descending.

So God, so Christ, so Jesus, so we. As Paul writes in 2 Corinthians, we carry in our bodies that same dying of Jesus, the same dissolving of the yeast.[16]

The prophetic songwriter Tom Conry wrote a very challenging liturgical text that some people found shocking: "We are called, we are chosen, we are Christ to one another."[viii]

16. 2 Cor 4:10.

Folks were kind of scandalized by that—"You can't say, 'We are Christ!'"—because this is not the kind of vocabulary we use very often in popular religiosity. But it was common vocabulary in the early centuries of Christianity. The fourth-century Coptic Christian monk and hermit Pseudo-Macarius, for example, taught that Jesus "was called Anointed (*Christos*) in order that we might receive the unction of the same oil with which he was anointed, and might thereby become 'christs' also, being of the same nature as he and forming a single body with him."[ix] Then he quotes the Letter to the Hebrews: "It is written likewise, *He who sanctified and those who are sanctified have all one origin.*"[17]

We are created in the image of God. In owning that, the next step is to move from image to likeness. How do we do that? Well, first of all we have to empty ourselves so that that image, covered over by layers of un-godliness, can shine through our humanity. The ascetical life starts there, and we set up the rest of our life in such a way as to ensure that we will keep that image clear and bright and unsullied. And then we move from image to likeness. Another ancient monastic writer, a fifth-century monk named Diadochus of Photike, expressed it this way: "All of us who are human beings are in the *image* of God. But to be in his *likeness* belongs only to those who by great love have attached their freedom to God."[x] Just as Jesus in love attached his freedom to his Abba, so we attach our freedom in love to Jesus, and to Jesus' way.

17. Heb 2:11.

And what was the way of Jesus? The way of God. The way of Christ. The way of emptiness.

stealing fire

Before we leave the Greek gods and the concept of power behind, let's look at another figure from that genre, Prometheus.

As my friends the D'Aulaires taught me when I was a boy, Prometheus was a minor god, a Titan. Zeus gave Prometheus and his brother Epimetheus the task of repopulating the earth after all living creatures had perished in an early battle of the gods. Prometheus was in charge of modeling all the humans, while Epimetheus was in charge of animals. Unfortunately, when Prometheus was done shaping the new humans he found that Epimetheus had already given all the best gifts to the animals—speed, sharp senses, and better endurance, as well as warm fur. So Prometheus asked Zeus if he could instead give the sacred fire to the humans. "But Zeus said no, fire belonged to the gods alone." So Prometheus, knowing he was risking great danger, decided to steal some fire from heaven, which he did, nabbing a glowing ember from the sacred hearth on Olympus and bringing it down to the humans, "and he told them never to let the fire from Olympus die out."

Well, Zeus was indeed furious. To add insult to injury Prometheus then also tricked Zeus, pulling a bait-and-switch with a burnt offering, giving the choicest parts of an ox to the people instead of to Zeus, and in doing so teaching the people how to cheat the gods. For his punishment Zeus had Prometheus chained to the top of a mountain where every day an eagle swooped out of the sky and ate his liver. Since he was immortal, every day his liver would grow back and the punishment was repeated endlessly.[xi]

Moderns and post-moderns have been captivated by this image of Prometheus stealing the fire from heaven, and have used it as a symbol of our grabbing power away from any kind of hierarchy and demagoguery. There is certainly something valid about that instinct and that energy, and many of the modern movements seem to be about this— feeling cheated out of the promise of liberation, and no one is going to give it to us if we don't own it and demand it and grab it. Certainly the woman's movement, now over a century in the making, is tied right into this energy. The entire sexual revolution, however misguided it might be at times and perhaps over-compensating, is actually a shaking off of the shackles of unhealthy inhuman Puritanism, Jansenism, and phobias of all kinds. The struggle for LGBT rights is really at its root the cry, "Let me live! Let us live!" No longer begging tolerance, but demanding the birthright— to live free. Is this not at the core of American values, enshrined in our Constitution, that we are "endowed by our Creator with the unalienable right to life, liberty and the pursuit of happiness"? The most obvious and perhaps purest example, of course, is the civil rights movement, rooted so deeply in the prophets of the Hebrew Scriptures.

I think here of two flags that in recent times have taken on a more sinister connotation but started out with the right spirit. The official flag of the state of New Hampshire contains the motto "Live free or die," a motto coming from the American and the French Revolutions. It might mean "I will die for my freedom," but it might also mean "I will die if I am not free." The other is the so-called Gadsden flag, the coiled rattlesnake with the words "Don't Tread on Me." It was again originally from the Revolutionary War and might have wound up the first flag of the United States, inspired by Benjamin Franklin, long before it was co-opted by racists.

So here in this story of Prometheus we see again the magical-mythical mindset about who the gods are—if not who God is—and who we are in relation to them. And if we think this is who our God is and what our God is like—that we have to steal the fire—then it is no wonder why at some point we rebel! We all have a moment when we feel like Prometheus, against this kind of God and against any kind of church that treads on me, limits my freedom, hordes power, and keeps the best for itself.

As a challenge to all that, however, we Christians have the story of Holy Thursday, and Christ Jesus, who did not deem equality with God, and divinity itself, something to be grasped at.

acted parables

The liturgist John Baldovin wrote that the Mass of the Lord's Supper on Holy Thursday centers on what he calls two "acted parables" that express the meaning of the death and resurrection of Jesus. One of course is the Eucharist. But before we approach the eucharistic table, almost overshadowing the table in its poignancy, comes the washing of the feet. Certainly on the Thursday before he died Jesus introduced this new ritual meal—"instituted the Eucharist" as we say—but if the church wanted us to remember just that or mainly that, she would have picked a reading from the Gospel of Matthew, Mark, or Luke, all of which tell the story of the actual words of institution. Instead, we read the Gospel of John—which never even mentions the meal. It recounts the startlingly tender and subservient ritual of Jesus washing his disciples' feet.

We find the liturgical rite of the washing of the feet as early as the fourth century, as a part of the baptismal rite in the western churches. It gradually disappeared but reemerged in the seventh century in Spain and Gaul when it began to be practiced by bishops and priests, and then showed up in the Roman liturgy by the twelfth century. According to the modern rubrics in the Roman rite it is to be performed by the priest presider on twelve men—*virii*, the Latin rubrics read. So imagine what a tizzy it threw the liturgists into on Holy Thursday 2013 when, right after he was elected, the photo was splashed on newspapers all over the world of Pope Francis washing the feet of prisoners in Rome. Not only not just priests; it was not just men, and it was not just Christians.

Ah, I thought to myself when I saw the photo, so this is how the church "seeks its mission in the profane world that surrounds it"; this is how the church "acts while disappearing." This is what it looks like for the church to go "beyond its confines" toward its separated Christian sisters and brothers, as well as to the Jewish people and non-Christians. This is what "the movement of a self-emptying of God and Christ" looks like, a "disinterested church" that doesn't seek its own glory, but the glory of its Lord, and union as love.[xii]

There's another practice that is meant to accompany the Holy Thursday liturgy. This is the only occasion in the course of the liturgical year that the Missal states that gifts for the poor are to be presented along with the gifts of bread and wine. Look at the beautiful parallels: Eucharist—footwashing: same thing. Gifts to the Lord—gifts to the poor: same thing. What is made visible is the connection between the Paschal Mystery, the life, passion, death and resurrection of Jesus, and the self-sacrifice of the church and its members. The recommended song for this time is the ancient text, "*Ubi caritas et amor Deus ibi es*"—"Where charity and love are found there is God."

Where there are charity and love—*that's* where God is. All three of these acts, footwashing, gifts for the poor, and Eucharist, Baldovin says, "ritually and symbolically express the fact that true life is to be found in the sacrifice of service." This is how we are to share the cross of Jesus and the kenosis of Christ—by laying our lives down in service, by doing as Jesus did. And this is made real in the symbolic act of footwashing by the president of the assembly. Jesus meant it literally when he said, "The greatest among you will be your servant. All who exalt themselves will be humbled, and all who humble themselves will be exalted."[18]

In America there has been a painful public debate about priests and other eucharistic ministers who think they have a right and a duty to deny Communion to certain people. The secular press has derisively referred to it as the "wafer wars." This denial of Communion, it must be said, has been particularly aimed at politicians who support keeping abortion legal. There are several problems with the hubris of such an act. First of all, as Psalm 130 sings, "If you, O LORD, should mark iniquities, / Lord, who could stand?"[19] This is in line with Pope Francis's well-known quote, "Who am I to judge?" just as St. Paul told the Romans, "you have no excuse, whoever you are, when you judge others."[20] As Joseph Ratzinger once wrote in an essay when he was still a young professor of theology, "Communion is not a prize

18. Matt 23:11-12.
19. Ps 130:3.
20. Rom 2.1.

for those who are particularly virtuous—who, in that case, could receive it without being a Pharisee?—but is instead the bread of pilgrims that God offers to us in this world, offers us in our weakness."[xiii]

In this context, if there were to be a litmus test or an entrance fee for receiving the Eucharist, it seems as apt as anything that the eucharistic minister should lean in to the communicant and whisper in his or her ear, "Did you wash anyone's feet today? Did you serve the poor? Did you offer your life in service as a sacrifice? Well done! Come to the table!"

Poder es Servir

Two other religious songs that were popular some years ago always come to my mind on Holy Thursday, two songs that differ from each other a bit.

The first one was written by a very talented Christian musician named Rich Mullins. It's called "Awesome God." The refrain goes like this:

Our God is an awesome God!
He reigns from heaven above
With wisdom, power, and love:
Our God is an awesome God!

And then the verses go on to describe some of God's actions in our world in the same vein:

When He rolls up His sleeves He ain't just putting on
    the Ritz.
There's thunder in His footsteps and lightning in
    His fists.
And the Lord wasn't joking when He kicked 'em out
    of Eden,
It wasn't for no reason that He shed His blood.
His return is very close and so you better be
    believin' that
Our God is an awesome God!

It's a very muscular rock anthem with an Old Testament image of God, a perfectly valid one. Zeus returns!

The other song I always think of on Holy Thursday was written by a liturgical musician named Bob Hurd. It's a bilingual song, in English and Spanish, entitled "Pan de Vida." It starts out in Spanish: "*Pan de Vida, cuerpo del Señor* (Bread of life, body of the Lord)"; then it goes to English: "Cup of blessing, blood of Christ the Lord." And in the next line he goes on to explain the *meaning* of the eucharistic gathering: "At this table the last shall be first"; and then there is the line that stays with me like a mantra on my lips, in my mind, and in my heart: "*Poder es servir, porque Dios es amor.*"

Power is to serve, because God is love.

Real power is in wrapping a towel around your waist and washing the feet of your friends.

power over and power with

This has some very practical real-life applications, for leaders all the way from heads of small communities to heads of state, and articulates what Jesus and the Christian tradition have to offer the conversation going on globally among nations and corporations. I attended a conference on leadership in religious community some years ago, and one of the most powerful images that was offered was the juxtaposition of and the difference between power *over* and power *with*, having power over someone or sharing power with someone. In some subtle but very enlightened way, this is really very practical: if you have power over me or if you exert power over me, I may do what you say as long as you're in the room, but as soon as you turn your back I'm going to get out from under your thumb and do whatever I want or whatever I think is best. You may win a couple of battles, but you won't necessarily win the war. On the other hand, if you share power with me or, even better, if you welcome *my* power alongside of yours, then you have won me over for life. Not only that, if you share power with me and welcome my power—what a tremendous force we are together!

If you get a sense of the tension in that you will suddenly realize that it affects not only how we approach leadership, but how we can understand almost everything in religion and spirituality. To some extent this is a both/and situation, but you will see right away where my prejudice lies and where the Gospel of Jesus tends.

In terms of God: I think that this is a notion that I only came to realize when I started studying the mystics. Yes, certainly our God is an awesome God, a God of power and might, and especially the Old Testament is replete with images of God having power over creatures and creation (and sometimes wiping out entire peoples who did nothing worse than be in the way). But there is another subtle strain of thought also running through our Scriptures, a theme of participation, meaning that God wants to *share* divine power with us. For example, 2 Peter, the clearest example, when Peter wishes that you "may become participants of the divine nature."[21] God is not just intent on having power over us. God wants us to share that power, as participants, as co-creators. "[M]ay we come to share in the divinity of Christ / who humbled himself to share in our humanity."

And this is certainly the image of God that we get from Jesus: "I do not call you servants any longer . . . but I have called you friends, because I have made known to you everything that I have heard from my Father."[22] He might as well have said, "I no longer want to have power over you; I want to share my power with you. I am the vine; you are the branches. This is how I have power over you; I tie an apron around my waist and wash your feet." There are no hidden meanings here. This is what it means to be the head of a family, a nation, an organization, a community—to be

21. 2 Pet 1:4.
22. John 15:15a.

a servant, and to share power with. *Poder es servir*, because God is love.

When Pope St. John Paul II visited Phoenix, the city where I was living some years ago, a woman I knew wrote an article for the local Catholic paper saying that she had experienced the whole church there at the gathering: the Church Militant—*Ecclesia Militans*, the Church Triumphant—*Ecclesia Triumphans*, and the *Ecclesia Penitens*, the Church Penitent or the Church Suffering. (Perhaps you will know of the famous fourteenth-century fresco of this by Andrea da Firenze in Santa Maria Novella in Florence.) I remember thinking even then, as I still think today, what about the Church Servant—*Ecclesia Servum*? Not that it hasn't always been in evidence to some extent throughout history, but this is obviously the face of the church that Pope Francis has wanted to be seen the most during his pontificate. I have often quoted Pope Paul VI in this regard, who, in his opening address to the second session of the Vatican Council, called on the church to change its attitude toward the modern world: "Not to despise but to appreciate, not to condemn but to comfort. Not to conquer but to serve."[xiv] *Poder es servir*, because God is love.

By the way, the songwriter Rich Mullins was a fine man, a great lover of Jesus, and a friend of a friend of mine. The song "Awesome God" was written early in his career as a contemporary Christian musician, but his later music was quite different. He grew to be very devoted to St. Francis of Assisi and spent the last years of his life living in a small hogan on a Navajo reservation in New Mexico where he taught music to children. I "met" him over the phone once and teased him about this very song lyric, a teasing that he took quite well—and returned. Once, after he moved onto the reservation, he was asked if he had made the move because God had called him to convert the Native Americans. He said no; he had just gotten "tired of a white, evangelical, middle-class perspective on God," and he thought he would "have more luck finding Christ among the pagan Navajos. I'm teaching music," he said. I think he had the heart of a real footwasher. He died tragically and way too young in a car accident in 1997.

fire on the earth

Thomas Merton, in a brilliant essay in the collection *Raids on the Unspeakable*, says that Christianity's answer to the fascination with Prometheus is that we actually believe, in spite of what we have somehow absorbed from our teachers, that our God wants to give us the fire! "I came to bring fire to the earth, and how I wish it were already kindled!" Jesus says.[23] We're trying to steal the fire from heaven, but the

23. Luke 12:49.

problem is we don't know where heaven is. It's not light years away in space. It's the very ground of our being and our consciousness; it's the fire in the heart of our heart. The irony is that the fire already blazes in each one of us, yet it is somehow the same fire of the Holy Spirit, the fire of divinity. It's even the fire of eros, the divine madness, the Greeks would call it, that we Christians believe God planted in us, our birthright, the divine creative energy.

What was the first sin, the primal flaw, the tragic mistake of Adam and Eve? Maybe it is only that they grasped at wisdom and life, they grabbed at it and were no longer content to receive it as a gift, the very opposite of Christ *not* clinging to divinity. So maybe the original sin is something like grabbing for power, like Prometheus. A little later in the Book of Genesis we hear the story of the Tower of Babel and it is almost the same dynamic, trying to build a ladder to climb to heaven, trying to storm the castle rather than be invited.

But the gift is not like the transgression, Paul says.[24] If the transgression—stealing the fire from heaven, eating of the forbidden tree—was in the jealous grasping, the gift is freely given. It can't be stolen and it can't be earned. And so we are back again to the great kenosis hymn. Christ Jesus does the opposite of Eve and Adam: he does not grab! Though his state was that of God yet he did not deem equality with God something that he should cling to, something

24. See Rom 5:15.

that he should grab at. Rather he emptied himself. He went back into his interdependency on God and the Spirit, and therefore God raised him on high and gave him the name above all other names. The gift is not like the offense. If the offense was grabbing and clinging and claiming, the gift is in Christ Jesus' emptying, trusting, receiving.

This does not mean that we blithely accept oppression, suppression, repression, injustice, servitude, but it does mean that real power and real freedom lie in being participants in the divine nature, the relationship with God that Jesus calls us to: "I am the vine, you are the branches."[25]

Of course, this then leads us to discern how this applies to all of our relationships. It's sort of counterintuitive, maybe especially for men, because power is the ultimate aphrodisiac, and so much in typical worldly affairs encourages us to believe that this is something to be sought—power over others, to be "king of the mountain," a CEO, to be the boss.

But Jesus says clearly, "It will not be so among you."[26]

what kind of seed?

Let's be realistic though. All this talk about God being merciful and forgiving does not mean that there are no

25. John 15:5.
26. Matt 20:26.

ramifications for evil. What we find out along the way, however, is that unrighteousness, like dysfunction, carries its own punishment. Worshiping other gods carries its own consequences. "Those who make them are like them; / so are all who trust in them."[27] There are consequences to our actions, for us and for our environment, for everything around us.

In the Gospel of Matthew, in his parable of the weeds and wheat, Jesus teaches that at harvest time the reapers will collect the weeds first and bind them in bundles to be burned, but the wheat will be gathered into the barn.[28] By our actions we can either be weeds or we can be wheat.

But let's go back a step: What is the *field* where these seeds get sown? The field is the world, Jesus tells us. And what is the seed? The good seed are the children of God— *we are* the seed. We are the seed that gets sown in the field of the world. And the wheat or weeds, which come up from the seed that is sown, are who we are and how we are in the world.

"The field is the world," Jesus explains to his disciples. In religion we are used to terminology that considers "the world" bad. In this case however, in this parable, "the world" itself is neutral—it's neither good nor bad. It's simply the field where the seed gets sown. It's the *seeds* that are good or bad. But actually—and I think this is important—if you

27. Ps 115:8.
28. Matt 13:24-30, 36-43.

look at Scripture, the story of creation from the Book of Genesis, for instance, the world isn't even neutral; it's actually good. That is one of the distinctive marks of the prophetic traditions, and especially of Judaism and Christianity. Whereas other religions (and Gnosticism and other heresies) might see the world as fallen or an illusion, our own canon of Scripture starts out with the story of a perfect being—God—creating a world on purpose, and then saying, "That's good. That's good." And (after creating the human being) "That's *really* good!" Jesus tells us that God is neither jealous of humans nor angry at the world in the way that we human beings get jealous or angry—or that Zeus and his cohorts do. As a matter of fact "God so loved the world that he gave his only Son . . ."[29] It is we who make the world—our world—good or bad by the seeds we sow, by the seeds we are.

At a very practical level, it's because we have been created in the image and likeness of God that we are the only creatures who have the ability to change God's perfect plan for creation, this good and beautiful world, as we have already done by changing the course of evolution, for instance—wiping out species, destroying entire ecosystems, and even changing the climate. So we might ask, are we, as a human race, good seed or bad seed?

29. John 3:16.

And so, who am I, how am I, in the world? Who am I in my environment? Am I a good seed or a bad seed? Am I turning out to be wheat or a weed? Do I sow division, gossip, cynicism, despair, pessimism, jealousy, contention, judgmentalism, or suspicion? Or do I sow the fruits of the Spirit that Paul lists in the Letter to the Galatians? Do I sow charity, joy, and peace? Do I sow patience, kindness, goodness, and generosity? Do I sow gentleness, faithfulness, modesty, self-control?[30] It's then that I am a good seed yielding wheat. This is the question: who are we and how are we in the world? Who am I, how am I in my world? We are reminded too of the Letter to James, while we're on the agricultural images: "a harvest of righteousness is sown in peace for those who make peace."[31]

What kind of seeds are we sowing? No, better yet: what kind of seed *are* we in this cruel, crazy, beautiful world?

In the Letter to the Corinthians Paul employs this same teaching regarding our other image of the reign of God, the yeast. We already are yeast in the dough, so what kind of yeast are we? This is a favored scriptural text for the Easter season, for the regeneration of our baptismal promises that is urged on us every year. "Do you not know that a little yeast leavens the whole batch of dough?" he says. So,

30. Gal 5:22-23.
31. Jas 3:18.

> Clean out the old yeast so that you may be a new batch, as you really are unleavened. . . . let us celebrate the festival, not with the old yeast, the yeast of malice and evil, but with the unleavened bread of sincerity and truth.[32]

Who am I, how am I, in the world? Who am I in my environment? Am I the old yeast or the unleavened bread of sincerity and truth?

paedagogos: humble in love

> Rivers and seas can master a hundred valleys
> because they lower themselves
> and thus become a hundred valleys' kings.
> Therefore those desiring a position above others
> must speak humbly.
> Those desiring to lead must follow.[33]

Ladders are a very common image in writings about the spiritual life, particularly in monastic literature, and they always seem to be climbing upward to heaven, such as the "Ladder of Divine Ascent" of the seventh-century abbot John Climacus of Sinai. To our surprise, however, we find that the ladder we climb to heaven actually goes down, down into our humanity, down to service, an ascent to the

32. 1 Cor 5:6-8.
33. *Tao te Ching,* #66.

depths of the heart. "Where charity and love are found, there is God."

This is the kind of leadership St. Benedict had in mind throughout his Rule for Monks. Saint Benedict says that the abbot should be loved more than feared, for example. Later in the Rule, Benedict quotes the First Letter of John: "There is no fear in love, but perfect love casts out fear; for fear has to do with punishment, and whoever fears has not reached perfection in love."[34] Poignantly, this is at the end of the chapter on the steps of humility. The way we get to perfect love is through humility.

Footwashing is mentioned three times in Benedict's Rule, not just as a necessity but as a ritual. And one of the mentions is in the reception of guests, and it is the abbot himself who is supposed to wash the feet of the newly arrived, greeting them as if they were Christ. And when he calls for bringing the brothers together for counsel (a monastic community is not necessarily a democracy, but it's certainly not a dictatorship either), he urges the abbot to listen even to the youngest members of the community.[35] "God descends, to the point of death on the cross . . . And we ascend to God by accompanying God on this descending path."

Poder es servir, because God is love.

34. 1 John 4:18.
35. RB 3; 72:7.

Just before I was elected prior of our community, I read through the very comprehensive fifty-five-page essay in the appendix of the RB 1980, the definitive modern translation and commentary on Benedict's Rule for Monks, regarding the abbot. According to the Rule, the prior of the monastery is actually the *second* in command under the abbot. But many of the reform traditions, especially hermit traditions such as ours, took off the top level during the medieval times, because abbots in those days were so often involved in economic and political intrigue. They preferred for their leaders to be more humble, a *primus intra pares*—the first among equals. But the qualities of an abbot still apply.

At any rate, the first part of the essay is about pre-Benedictine practice and not necessarily about leaders of monastic communities, while the second part is all about the understanding of the abbot from St. Benedict on. I actually read the second part first and then came back to the first part. Not much in the second part had really touched me—mostly it just intimidated me! The only other real experience of a monastery I had had before was at an archabbey, and their archabbot wore a pectoral cross and a ring, and was surrounded by copious high ceremony and formality. Then I went back and read through the first part of the essay, which was about spiritual fatherhood in the Scriptures, about the *abbas* of the desert and other early monastic communities of Egypt, and the early monastic experiments in Cappadocia.

Right at the very end of that section I found an image from the fourth-century Cappadocian mystical writer

Gregory of Nyssa that struck me deeply. It's from a treatise entitled *On the Christian Mode of Life*. When Gregory writes about the obligations of leaders, those who are "in charge," he does not compare them to a father. He doesn't use the word *abba*; he uses the Greek word *paedagogos*, and says the leader of a Christian community ought to be a *paedagogos*. Sometimes that word gets translated as a "skilled educator," but actually in ancient times among wealthy families the *paedagogos* was a slave that the parents hired to instruct the children. And that's what the leader of a Christian community, a Christian family, ought to be—a *paedagogos*.

I thought that was beautiful and, obviously, very much in keeping with the gospel. In the Rule of Benedict, even as in some other earlier Christian writings, there can be a kind of mixed metaphor of Trinitarian language; Jesus himself is sometimes referred to as a father. But Clement of Alexandria, for instance, refers instead to Christ mainly as a *paedagogos*. Jesus, instead of being a Promethean character stealing the fire from heaven and bringing it down to mortals, is the slave whom the Father has entrusted with the task of instructing the children. Two biblical references come to mind. The first is Matthew 23:9, when Jesus himself says, "Call no one your father on earth, for you have one Father—the one in heaven." And then again Paul's great kenosis hymn in the Letter to the Philippians, that Jesus did not deem equality with God something to be grasped at but emptied himself and took the form of a slave—could we say that he took the form of a *paedagogos*?—and humbled himself, obediently accepting death, even death on a cross.

humble obedience

Actually, this same attitude of humility is one of the hallmarks of *any* monk as far as St. Benedict is concerned, not just the abbot. Benedict devotes one whole long, very difficult chapter (7) to what he calls the 12 Steps of Humility. Right at the beginning of the chapter he quotes the Gospel of Luke: "Those who exalt themselves will be humbled, and those who humble themselves will be exalted."[36] The language that Benedict uses is very hard, even shocking, for us moderns to hear, especially when so many have been wounded by hierarchical abuse and family dysfunction, and trained in the language of emotional intelligence or recovery. But still, there it is: St. Benedict asks his monks to quietly embrace suffering, even in difficult and unjust conditions, to be content with the lowliest treatment, and, especially, to be convinced that you are inferior to all. Of course, we have to keep in mind here the crucified Jesus and the Suffering Servant, but even for a mature person all that also has to be put in the context of a real, sturdy, mature ego as well as a healthy image of God.

36. Luke 14:11, 18:14; RB 4:1.

The other steps are a little easier to nuance and contextualize, for example, remembering that God is always watching, which goes along with not concealing sinful thoughts from your spiritual father—rigorous honesty. "Who am I to judge?" If I look at how hard I have struggled in my own life with all the help I've had, it should be easy to be humble or at least not to be proud or arrogant or judgmental. Benedict also tells his monks that they should manifest humility in their bearing no less than in their heart—which includes things like controlling the tongue, not being given to ready laughter, and speaking gently—so that one's humility is evident everywhere, at liturgy, on a journey, in the garden, in a field. (This of course cannot possibly mean that we are just supposed to put on a show, *ad oculos*—for everyone to see how humble we are, since Jesus warns about that as well.[37])

But I think the real key is in the admonition that we find in the second and third step of humility: to love not your own will—just as Jesus says of himself, "I have come down from heaven, not to do my own will, but the will of him who sent me."[38] For the monk that means to submit to legitimate authority, and to do nothing but what is endorsed by the common rule of the monastery and by *conversatio*. Saint Benedict makes a big point of this throughout the

---

37. See Matt 6:16.
38. John 6:38.

Rule, tying humility to obedience as if they go together and together form the basis for all monastic life.

But obedience isn't just obedience to the abbot or to the Rule, and this is where I think we get some real clarity. Benedict names an entire chapter (71) *Ut oboedientes sibi sunt invicem*—"That they may obey one another"! He says that "Obedience is a blessing to be shown by all, not only to the abbot but also to one another as brothers and sisters." And then, in the next chapter, he cites Romans 12:10, urging that they should each try to be the first to show respect to the other, "supporting with the greatest patience one another's weaknesses of body and behavior, and earnestly competing in obedience to one another. No one is to pursue what they judge best for themself, but instead what they judge better for someone else." That's real humility. It's tied to obedience, tied to service, tied to charity. This is the hallmark of a Christian monastic community—that we are each a *paedagogos*. And ultimately this is not a negative thing; it's positive. Humility means I care about you over me. Humility means loving your neighbor as yourself.

So, not just humility, but humble obedience, even mutual obedience.

But I want to go one step further and say that this is not just about the *monastic* impulse: the Christian impulse itself is marked by this tendency, this positive kind of humility. It applies to a parent, a nurse, a laborer, a cook. In that same essay by Gregory of Nyssa, before he writes about the leaders he is writing about everyday Christians. They should be "ready to do whatever is confided to them with hope and eagerness; they will do it as Christ's servants for the good of the brothers and sisters." Then he too quotes the gospel: "let them take the last place and be the servants of all." "Such persons must be subject to all others and serve their brothers and sisters as though they were their debtors."[xv] It's all more positive than negative, not so much about walking around looking humble and much more about our stance in the world as a follower of Jesus' way, as an imitator of Jesus—being a servant. Not just humble—humble servants.

be perfect, be merciful

In Matthew's version of the Sermon on the Mount Jesus says, "You have heard that it was said, 'An eye for an eye and a tooth for a tooth'" (which is actually quoting Exod 21:24 and Lev 24:19), "but I say to you . . ."[39] That's called the law of retaliation. We might think that sounds harsh, but even that is actually an advance over other primitive societies, an advance in the evolution of the moral conscience, you might say. Before that particular way of thinking there was only reprisal and retribution, revenge and vengeance, even sanctioned in the Bible! "An eye for an eye" is at least proportional; it limits reprisal to reciprocity,

39. Matt 5:38-39.

hence, an eye for an eye—and no more. "Vengeance is mine," says the Lord.[40]

But in later Jewish thought there is also what is sometimes called the Silver Rule, as opposed to the Golden Rule: "Do not do unto others what you would not have them do unto you," intimated already in the Book of Tobit and found in the teachings of the great Jewish teacher Hillel, who was a near contemporary of Jesus. But then of course comes the Golden Rule, which asks for a little more, or asks for the same thing in a positive light: "In everything do to others as you would have them do to you."[41] This "rule" implies positive action; it takes the initiative to create an atmosphere of good will.

And then comes the next step, Jesus' teaching, "Love your enemies and pray for those who persecute you."[42] This is nothing less than moral heroism; this is the height of sanctity, this is perfection.

This also of course is a challenge to the language that we use nowadays when speaking about war, and one of the debates about nuclear weapons and "proportional response." (In a nuclear age can there even be such a thing as a proportional response?) Jesus takes us a step beyond proportional response, and you can see how easy it is to make a case for absolute pacifism. "But I say to you, love your

40. Deut 32:35.
41. Matt 7:12.
42. Matt 5:44.

enemies . . . " This next step is no retribution at all, sur-
rendering even your lawful rights for the sake of charity,
for the sake of mercy. The folks that work in what's called
restorative justice are a lot closer to the gospel injunctions
than anything else, meaning the proper response to a crime
or to an injustice is to heal the relationship; the proper
response is always reconciliation. "Love your enemies, and
pray for those who persecute you."

So what is Jesus the good Jewish teacher doing? He is
bringing the law to its fulfillment as he has said earlier in
the same sermon: "Do not think that I have come to abol-
ish the law . . . but to fulfill [it]."[43] A few sentences later
Matthew uses the Greek word *teleios*—perfect: "Be perfect,
therefore, as your heavenly Father is perfect."[44] It's related
to the Greek word *telos*, which means the end, the ultimate
goal: to be perfect is to have reached the consummated goal
of life. You could say Jesus is bringing the law to its *telos*—
to its end, its consummated goal, and its fulfillment. And
what does it mean to be perfect? What's the fulfillment of
the law?

There are several variations on this saying, and perhaps
they all come together in Jesus. The Book of Deuteronomy
urges us to be blameless (*tamin*); in the Book of Leviticus
the admonition is to be *qedosim*—"be holy as I am holy." As
we noted, Matthew uses the word *teleios*, usually translated

43. Matt 5:17.
44. Matt 5:48.

"perfect." To the Greek mind to be perfect meant being con-
formed to the divine ideal. And that's where the Gospel of
Luke comes in handy and ties it back to this teaching about
our enemies: in Luke's version of this story Jesus says, "Be
merciful, just as your heavenly Father is merciful."[45]

That's what it means to be perfect—it means to be merciful. That is what conforms to the divine ideal. That's what
it means to be like God who rains on the just and the unjust.
"Love your enemies, and pray for those who persecute you."
We might think our *telos*, our ultimate goal, is union with
God, or a stilled mind, or saying our mantra for a half an
hour without interruption, or my body dying and my soul
going to heaven. But Jesus tells us that our ultimate goal is
to be merciful as God is merciful. That is the proof of our
perfection. The fulfillment of the law is mercy.

The Jewish Scriptures still allow praying for the defeat of
our enemy, but, with all due respect, we Christians are not
allowed to do that anymore. (I would also hasten to add that
of all the rabbis I have met or worked with I can't imagine
one of them encouraging praying for vengeance or violence
against their foes.) A big debate had begun once we Catholics
started praying the psalms in English instead of Latin after
the Second Vatican Council, about whether or not we could
use the so-called "cursing psalms." There was a school of
thought in the ancient monastic tradition that we were really

45. Luke 6:36.

cursing the demons or the *logismoi* (evil thoughts) and not our neighbors in those cursing psalms. However, it is pretty hard to explain that to people when you are singing, in public liturgy, "O God, break the teeth in their mouths; / . . . like grass let them be trodden down and wither. / Let them be like the snail that dissolves into slime; / like the untimely birth that never sees the sun"[46]—as Psalm 58 does, even if it is being sung sweetly, in Gregorian chant.

No, many Scripture scholars and liturgists said very clearly, "These are not Christian prayers!" We have to make a real selective use of the things that we say publicly. And we do: there are psalms that never get used in public worship in the Catholic tradition. Our monastic community opted not even to sing some of the lines from Psalm 136, the litany that sings the praises of God whose "steadfast love endures forever," but who also "struck Egypt through their firstborn, / . . . who struck down great kings, / . . . and killed famous kings."[47] I used to think, "What if a non-Christian Egyptian suddenly popped into church while we were singing that?!"

Jesus is pretty clear about a few things, and one of them is to pray for your enemy, to love your enemy, to bless and *do not curse them*! Imagine Jesus teaching this to his contemporary co-religionists, who were no doubt familiar with calling down scriptural curses on their enemies, on their

46. Ps 58:6-8.
47. Ps 136:10, 17-18.

Roman occupiers, or even on their neighbor who had stolen their property. Love your enemy, be like God, be perfect, be merciful. To be perfect like God is to be merciful like God. Mercy is perfection. Be like God. Be perfect. Be merciful. No exceptions.

There is no place in the gospel for revenge, reprisal, retaliation—only mercy, only restoration, only reconciliation.

Jesus didn't just die for the persecuted; he also died for the persecutors. This is a new kind of justice, one rooted in mercy, one that breaks the vicious cycle of hate and revenge, and forms both the persecuted and the persecutors together into a new humanity. And that's what we are called to do and to be in this violent world too, we followers of Jesus, the ones who finally break the vicious cycle of hatred and revenge. That applies to our petty little squabbles as well as to our grand gestures. We are the ones who choose to be in the front line of this way of being human.

This too is our kenosis.

The Book of Deuteronomy says that we must observe these statutes and decrees with all our heart and all our soul.[48] We are to be a people peculiarly God's own. Deuteronomy is applying this to the strictures and codes of the law, but when we Christians hear it, we hear this admonition on the lips of Jesus concerning his own teaching. "You

---

48. Deut 26:16.

must observe these statutes and decrees with all your heart and all your soul: *Be perfect. Be merciful.* No exceptions."

Saint Benedict thought this was a pretty important teaching for his monks too. This is from Chapter 4 of the Rule:

> Live by God's commandments every day . . .
> harbor neither hatred nor jealousy of anyone,
> and do nothing out of envy.
> Do not love quarreling; shun arrogance.
> Respect the elders and love the young.
> Pray for your enemies out of love for Christ.
> If you have a dispute with someone,
> make peace with them before the sun goes down.
> And finally, never lose hope in God's mercy.[49]

Dominionism

> Giving birth, nourishing life,
> shaping things without possessing them,
> serving without expectation of reward,
> leading without dominating:
> These are the profound virtues of nature,
> and of nature's best beings.[50]

49. RB 4:63-74.
50. *Tao Te Ching*, 51.

There is a school of thought that has been surfacing in the American political realm known as "Dominionism." The philosophy basically holds that Christians (and Christians alone!) are biblically mandated to occupy all secular institutions until Jesus returns.[xvi] Some of these Dominionists, like the late Francis Shaeffer, who is singled out as the main inspirer of this movement, even argue for violent overthrow of governments—in the name of the Bible! Dominionism relies on Genesis 1:28, where human beings are urged to "fill the earth and subdue it; and have dominion . . . over every living thing that moves upon the earth."[51]

But it seems to me that the texts Christians should be looking at for *how* we are supposed to have dominion in the world are the ones we have already looked at: "The greatest among you must be your servant." Or the Philippians canticle that says Christ Jesus emptied himself and took the form of a slave. Or else John 13, which shows exactly how Jesus had dominion: he tied a towel around his waist and washed his disciples' feet! That's how we are supposed to have dominion over the earth. We are supposed to be the slaves even of the fish and the fowl and the cattle; we are supposed to be servants of every creeping thing that creeps upon the earth; we are supposed to wash the feet of all others, not be their masters.

51. Gen 1:28.

It's not just the monastic movement or religious life, but the Christian movement itself that is marked by this tendency toward poverty and powerlessness. And it's not just the Christian movement either, but the spiritual life itself that is marked by this movement toward dispossession and a "blessed simplicity," as Raimundo Panikkar titled his famous book on the monastic movement. Notice the quote from the *Tao Te Ching* above. This is a universal teaching, a part of the perennial philosophy.

the struggle against the self

The famous *hadith* of the Prophet Mohammed comes to mind. He had dispatched a contingent of the army to the battlefront, and when they returned he said to them,

> "Blessed are those who have performed the minor *jihad* and have yet to perform the greater *jihad*." When asked, "What is the greater *jihad*?" the Prophet replied: "The *jihad* of the self."[xvii]

In Arabic this is known as *jihad al-nafs*, the "struggle against the self." (The Arabic word *nafs* is related to the Hebrew word *nepesh*, sometimes translated as "soul.") This struggle against the self is really against evil ideas, desires, and the powers of lust, anger, and insatiable imagination, placing them all under the dictates of reason and faith in obedience to God's command, and finally purging all evil ideas and influences from one's soul. Having dominion over these is much more difficult than fighting on the battlefield. In his encyclical *Spe Salvi*, Pope Benedict asks, "Are we not perhaps seeing once again, in the light of current history, that no positive world order can prosper where souls are overgrown?"[xviii] Otherwise, how often have we seen religion turned into a kind of tribal warfare? Recall Abraham Lincoln's warning against presuming that God is on our side, but rather humbly praying every day that we are on God's side.

We have to be constantly vigilant and swim against the stream, because without our noticing it what we started out to do can become its polar opposite.

And let's take one more step here, too, in regard also to nature. I'm not exactly sure how we Christians are supposed to understand the biblical injunction to "fill the earth and subdue it; and have dominion . . . over every living thing that moves upon the earth" except to say that here too we are supposed to exercise dominion the same way Jesus exercised dominion: we put on an apron and we serve, like a steward, a servant. In fact Pope Francis pointed out that having dominion is only one of the models of our relationship with nature as presented in the Book of Genesis. There is also stewardship, which is different than dominion. But if we fast forward much further ahead we come to St. Francis of Assisi, who called the elements his siblings! Brother Sun, Sister Moon, Brother Fire, our light at night, Sister Water so lowly. Are we here too more like *primes intra pares*—first among equals?

Again, this is very practical wisdom. In the big picture, if we keep on trying to subdue the earth, if we keep trying to have power over the earth the way we have been since at least the rise of the Industrial Age, we may win a couple more battles, but we are totally going to lose the war. The earth is eventually going to win this one. All she has to do is get rid of this pesky annoying human species, once we ourselves have made the planet uninhabitable for human beings, and she will regenerate just fine. But if, like Anthony of the Desert or Francis of Assisi, we could finally learn to *share* the power of the earth, us offering earth our voice, our power of adaptation and intellection, and earth like a mother lovingly sharing all her powers and forces of creativity with us, it would be like flying on the wings of an eagle, or riding on the back of a mighty stallion, working with the natural powers and gifts of creation to bear fruit abundantly, with more than enough for everyone.

The late Franciscan Benedict Groeschel, who was no tree-hugging liberal, speaking of the sacramental world in his classic book *Spiritual Passages*, suggested that those in the illuminative way are intuitive environmentalists. "One can hardly imagine a spiritual person consciously despoiling the environment or lacking a sensitivity to beauty, which is one of the voices of God," he says.[xix]

Poder es servir, because God is love.

Actually, I wonder if this couldn't apply to our own bodies as well, and the natural power of generativity that flows through our veins. The *jihad al-nafs*, the conquering of and dominion over our physical self, is not so much to have power *over* it as to be able to work with it, to channel it, focus it like a laser, into all kinds of procreativity. This is one of the areas where the holistic Asian philosophies and practices have appeared very attractive to our fractured Western European Greek-influenced dualism that constantly wants to subdue the body or cast it off completely in a kind of punitive asceticism. How utterly strange for a religious tradition rooted in God-becoming-flesh! No, better to exercise love, even if tough love, on the body, the love of a *paedagogos* who is answerable to a higher power for how we have treated the gift of our bodies. Remember that St. Francis himself apologized to his own body as he lay dying—"Brother Ass" he called it—for having treated it so badly.

The simple gesture of washing feet is really an icon of a whole attitude and outlook on life. It may look like weakness, but really it takes nothing less than heroic strength and dedication, a love as "strong as death," "fierce as the grave,"[52] having "the same mind that was in Christ Jesus, who, though he was in the form of God, did not deem equality with God something to be grasped at. Rather he emptied himself, took the form of a slave."[53]

---

52. Song 8:6.
53. See Phil 2:5-7.

our joy is heaven's mirth

At the same time, we have to be careful not to fall into some kind of self-annihilation in the name of holiness nor a purely penitential asceticism as perhaps some former generations of Christians did, thus giving a bad name to Christian asceticism in general.

I'm always torn between two approaches to the will, for instance. On the one hand, there is the "stout stubborn will" that is "up and doing," and there is free will and willpower, and there is the love that is an act of the will when it doesn't feel good anymore. And yet at some point we have to have the crisis of realizing the limitation of our willpower. Paul speaks of it in Romans 7:

> I do not do what I want, but I do the very thing I hate. Now if I do not do what I want . . . in fact it is no longer I that do it, but sin that dwells in me. . . . I delight in the law of God in my inmost self, but I see in my members another law at war with the law of my mind, making me captive to the law of sin that dwells in my members. Wretched man that I am! Who will rescue me from this body of death?[54]

There's a very subtle anthropological and moral argument at work here. I have spent enough hours on either side of

---

54. Rom 7:15-16, 20, 22-24.

the confessional to know how true this is about the sins we confess: We keep doing things that we hate to do! But, Paul teaches, it's not really we who do it—our inner self actually agrees with the law of God. It's some darkness that dwells in us. There is actually something optimistic about this passage, hopeful, with a positive view of human nature: my inner self agrees with the law of God! (This is the argument for natural law, by the way, which is also based on Paul's Letter to the Romans, chapter 2: "When Gentiles, who do not possess the law, do instinctively what the law requires . . . [t]hey show that what the law requires is written on their hearts."[55]) It may be a deep dig to find that deepest part of ourselves, our innermost self that agrees with the law of God, but it seems well worth the effort.

But the text doesn't end with Paul saying, "Wretched man that I am!" It ends with Paul crying out, "Who will rescue me . . . ? Thanks be to God through Jesus Christ our Lord!" Paul's point is—and what many people, especially those who struggle with addictions, have discovered—that we can call on a Power-Greater-Than-Ourselves. There is spiritual power, a divine power, to which we have access by calling on the name of Jesus, our compassionate high priest. This Power can come from outside of us—from "above"—but this power is also within us, our innermost self that agrees with the law of God, that deepest part of us where, as Paul writes earlier in Romans, the love of God

55. Rom 2:14-15.

has been "poured into our hearts" by the Spirit living in us. That, he says, is why hope does not disappoint us, because the love of God is the ground of our being. If we feel trapped in anything, from our petty compulsivities to our life-stultifying addictions, from our misdemeanors to our high crimes, if we find that we keep on doing things we hate to do, there is hope. There is power available to us by calling out and by reaching in.

It's a dire mistake to think that we can achieve salvation or enlightenment based solely on our own willpower. Paul says it just can't be done. We have to discover this to achieve any kind of progress in the spiritual life, the gap between our will and our concrete reality. As a wise man once explained to me, it's like a ladder that goes to the moon. We climb to the top of the ladder by the power of our will, but when we get to the top we find that we are still 238,899 miles away from the moon. The rest of the way is all grace. We don't really learn to ask for mercy until we experience this poverty.

the will

This leads me to think that perhaps our own will is not the problem at all. Our will isn't something evil: it's just not enough. That's the problem! Paul says our innermost being desires the good; as the psalmist says, "I delight to do your will, O my God; / your law is within my heart."[56] (Perhaps

---

56. Ps 40:8.

a better translation of this, closer to the original Hebrew, might be, "I carry your law in the depths of my bowels.") My deepest self delights in your law. That's my real "will." It's just not enough—my own will. Psalm 40:6-8 reminds us that it's not enough to offer sacrifices, either, as we might to appease the gods.

> Sacrifice and offering you do not desire,
>   but you have given me an open ear.
> Burnt offering and sin offering
>   you have not required.
> Then I said, "Here I am;
>   in the scroll of the book it is written of me.
> I delight to do your will, O my God;
>   your law is within my heart."

We need, perhaps, to be emptied even of the ability to offer sacrifices except for the sacrifice of a humble heart.

The problem with this emptying is that we might be tempted to believe that God's will somehow means our annihilation, that this emptying means our annihilation. I was speaking to a very pious young woman once who told me that she didn't know what to do with her life. She had, she said, spent so many years doing what she thought would make her happy, and now she wanted to do God's will. And it struck me that maybe they weren't two different things, God's will and her will, her joy. I recall a scene from the movie "Chariots of Fire." The protagonists are two long distance runners. One of the two runners is a young, pious man from a devout Christian missionary family as well as being a very talented athlete. Most of his family, especially his sister, thinks he no longer cares about God with all this running business. He is very torn himself, but he just can't seem to stop. Finally, in one climatic scene he says to his sister, "I believe that God made me for a purpose. But he also made me fast, and when I run, I feel his pleasure."

There is a deep truth there: God's joy is our delight; God's will is our pleasure. *Gratia non tollit naturam, sed perfecit*, St. Thomas Aquinas taught: Grace does not destroy our nature, but perfects it. Grace is the source of our nature, grace builds on our will—it's not the annihilation of it. As Pope St. Leo the Great said about the incarnation, just as God does not change by condescension, just as the Word does not lose equality with the Father's glory by becoming flesh, so humanity is not swallowed up by being exalted, flesh does not leave behind the nature of our race. Jesus wasn't annihilated, even at death. He died, yes, but the whole point of the resurrection is that even death is not an annihilation. He was raised body and soul to the right hand of glory. Not a nameless, faceless nothing, not a drop of water re-emerging into the ocean—his *very person* exists!

When we are emptied of everything vestigial we will find that our innermost self, our deepest and truest self, delights in the law of God because our truest self is a reflection of the glory of God, an image of God. When I am really me, my truest self, I am a reflection of the beautiful image of the Divine. So perhaps it's not our own will that needs to be demolished, but these other things that have a will of their own and are taking up space rent free inside of us: the tyranny of the false self, the tyranny of sin and addiction, the tyranny of disordered emotions and memories and regrets that lead us to compulsively bury ourselves under layers upon layers of noise or isolation, or hide behind masks and defenses, and in doing so hide not only from the rest of humanity, but hide even from ourselves and ultimately from God's will, which actually is written on our hearts, buried under all that junk.

Meister Eckhart said, "I never ask God to give himself to me: I beg him to purify me, empty me. If I am empty, God of his very nature is obliged to give himself to me."[xx] When the Spirit allows us clean hands and a pure heart and tranquil minds, we will be nothing but the glory of God, the Word taking flesh in the fertile garden of our depths. That's God's will.

As Frederich Buechner wrote in *Wishful Thinking*, concerning vocation, "The place God calls you is where your deep gladness meets the world's deep hunger." There is an important truth there: God's joy is our delight; God's will is our pleasure. Or, as Thomas Merton ended his wonderful meditation on Prometheus, "There is nothing we can steal from Him at all, because before we can think of stealing it, it has already been given."[xxi] That's why we don't have to steal the fire from heaven, like Prometheus: God gives us the fire. Grace builds on nature, grace is the source of our nature, grace builds on our will. All we need to do is empty ourselves of all that is not godly, of all that is not really us. When we are empty, God of his very nature is obliged to give himself to us. Merton echoed Meister Eckhart when he wrote that "God loves and helps best those who are so beat and have so much nothing but had gradually lost everything, piece by piece, until there is nothing left but God."[xxii]

the obscuring ego

> Unless one is completely annihilated
> Union is not a reality.
> Union is not the merging of spirits;
> the secret of Union
> is the annihilation itself.
>
> *Rumi*[xxiii]

The great spiritual teacher Bede Griffiths, an English monk who spent the last decades of his life on a Christian ashram in India, said once that he thought the key to the spiritual life was not even stripping away or destroying or killing or annihilating the ego, but simply recognizing how much we are *influenced* by the ego. The ego is a good thing, a marvelous function of our psyche. The problem is the wounded and unhealthy ego, when it becomes bloated and inflated. The more inflated it becomes, the more it prevents things from coming in and from coming out. It also prevents us from looking within, because it gets so bloated and self-important that we start to believe our own advertising, what Merton called our "false self." That's ego-*ism*.

In tenth-century Iran there was a Sufi mystic named al-Junayd who is credited with mapping out the ground of all future Islamic mysticism. He wrote beautifully about a mysterious concept in Sufism known as ʿfanā. It is usually translated as "annihilation," annihilation of the self or of the ego, though some argue that that is too strong of a word. The basis of the teaching is that if and when we strip away our obscuring egoism we discover the divine presence at the heart of our own being. This experience then gives us greater self-realization and self-control, and we become more human. What we are really returning to is our own primordial state, to the ideal human-ness that God intended all along. I like to think of this, combining a phrase made famous by Merton and one drawn from Paul's Letter to the Colossians, as our "real self hidden with Christ in God."[57]

We have a similar optimism in Christian mystical theology, that as we gaze on Christ Jesus, we discover the very pattern of humanity and, as St. John tells us, when we see him as he is, "we will be like him."[58] Jesus is the very image of God, and we are an image of that image. And if and when we strip away the obscuring egoism, we discover that image. We discover what Jeremiah prophesied, that the law is writ-

57. See Col 3.3.
58. 1 John 3:2.

ten on our hearts.[59] (This is the very passage that Paul quotes
in the letter to the Romans when he shows that the written
law will not save, because even Gentiles who do not know
the law can have and display an innate sense of uprightness.)[60]

As hard as it is, we simply must believe that there is
freedom here in this way, in the kenosis of Jesus, this stripping away of the egoism that obscures our vision of reality
inside and out, in this discovery of the divine presence, the
love of God, at the heart of our own being, this image of
God at the Source, *as* the Source, of our own being, this law
written on our hearts. In following the way of Jesus, this is
where we are led, to our own hearts, to this truth, the truth
of who we truly are—and that is the truth that can set us
free.

de-construct yourself

I want to tell you about the charism of my own monastic congregation, the Camaldolese. Put briefly, we are an eleventh-
century reform of Benedictine monasticism. Most Christian
monks in Europe at that time were what we call "cenobites,"
which basically means they lived in community, a contemplative life of praying, working, and studying together. (Those are
the three pillars of Benedictine monastic life—prayer, work,
and study.) But our founder, the tenth-century St. Romuald

59. Jer 31:33.
60. Jer 31:33; Rom 2:15.

of Ravenna, intentionally, specifically added, as I like to say, two wings to the body of monasticism.

Let's say the body is community life. First of all, St. Romuald brought in the possibility of living in greater and greater solitude, a type of monasticism that was very common in the early days of Christianity, especially in the deserts of Egypt, with the possibility even of living as a recluse with virtually no communal life of prayer or work or socializing. That is what Romuald is mostly known for, as being "the father of the sensible hermits who live under the Rule." But some of our early monks were also missionary martyrs (and I specifically put those two words together— not just missionaries, not just martyrs, but missionary martyrs). They went into lands that were at the time still hostile among barbarian tribes, Poland and Hungary (as hard to imagine as that might be now), and they were killed for it.

And so from the earliest days of our congregation we have had what is called the Threefold Good, the *triplex bonum*: community, solitude, and this third thing, which we don't like to name, but it was originally missionary martyrdom. We tend to think of this third good now as total self-donation, absolute availability to the Spirit. At times even reclusion—total solitude—was considered to be the equivalent of martyrdom, as the ancients would say, a "white martyrdom" instead of a "red martyrdom."

The reason I bring that up is that there was a document discovered only in the late nineteenth century that contains two writings that our monks had lost for centuries. It's called "The Life of the Five Brothers," and it's the story of the first monks who went off to foreign lands and were martyred. Mind you, these monks were not doing any kind of active evangelization. They were merely living their contemplative life in the midst of a hostile people, thinking that the witness of their life would be enough.

First of all, in that document, "The Life of the Five Brothers," this threefold good is named very succinctly: ". . . a nice *cenobium* for those newly come from the world, golden solitude for the mature members thirsting for the living God, and the preaching of the Gospel . . . for those eager to *depart* and be with Christ." What I am focusing on is that word "depart." It's a phrase from St. Paul's Letter to the Philippians[61] when he is speaking of his approaching death, and he says, "my desire is to depart and be with Christ, for that is far better." But what I found interesting is that the Latin phrase used in "The Life of the Five Brothers" is *cupientibus dissolvi et esse cum Christo*—eager to *dissolve* and be with Christ, not "depart." The Latin is *dissolvi*, to "dissolve or break apart," which our Italian monks also translate as *sciogliersi*—"to break apart or loosen."[xxiv] Our expert translator warned me I might be seeing too much into this, but I love this notion and have been savoring it like a mantra: I'm not really longing for death to go

61. Phil 1:23.

to heaven so much as I want to dissolve to be with Christ—
even in this life.

The other writing that is contained in "The Life of the
Five Brothers" is what is known as "The Brief Rule of Saint
Romuald." It is the only writing that we know of from the
great saint, so we cherish it. It's basically a rule for the other
wing, for the hermit, for the solitary, and it has two famous
lines in it. The first is the opening line: "Sit in your cell as
if in Paradise." And the other is toward the end. It is usually
translated as "Empty yourself completely and sit waiting,
content with the grace of God," which is quite an attractive
phrase. Another very fine translator used a stronger word
in his translation: "*Destroy* yourself completely and sit waiting . . ." So again I went back and looked at both the Latin
and the Italian.[xxv]

The Latin is *destrue*, which the Italians translate as *an-
ientati*—"annihilate yourself"! In speaking with our lin-
guists, I've come to think that something between "empty"
and "destroy" is probably best, and if it weren't so awkward
and un-poetic we might want to say something like, "deconstruct yourself completely and sit waiting, content with
the grace of God." The opposite of building up a self: deconstruct yourself. Dissolve. Like a seed. Like yeast. Like
salt.

My point is that the advice to the solitary hermit is basically the same as the advice to the missionary—to forget
the self, to go beyond the self, to let the self dissolve, to
deconstruct this false self that we have built up and/or let

be built up around us. Perhaps in between the two is Paul's other famous phrase, "it is no longer I who live, but it is Christ who lives in me."[62] Or the phrase from the Third Step Prayer of AA that asks to be "relieved of the bondage of self." If we are relieved of the bondage of self, we can be totally available to the Spirit.

I found those exact words "bondage of self" echoed in a translation of the fifteenth-century Sufi poet Jāmī: "Although you may attempt to do a hundred things in this world, only Love will give you release from the bondage of yourself."[xxvi] This love is very important, because this process doesn't end in *fanā*, destruction or annihilation. According to Sufi teaching, *fanā* is followed by *baqā*—a revival, a re-vivification, a return to the self, but a return to an enhanced self.

A. J. Arberry, a scholar of Sufism, describes *baqā* instead as "continuance." And he explains that by passing away from self, mystics don't cease to exist as an individual, in the true sense of existence. Instead what happens is that "one's individuality, which is an inalienable gift from God, is perfected, transmuted and eternalized through God and in God." Echoing Paul's sentiments—that he would rather depart to be with God—the return to continued existence becomes a source of trial (*balā*) and affliction, "for we are still apart and veiled from God." And so Sufi poets, like the author of the Song of Songs, use the imagery of the lover

---

62. Gal 2:20.

yearning for the beloved, all the while, paradoxically, "taking intense joy in the suffering which this separation causes."[xxvii] It is this dual sense of union and separation that many of the Sufi mystics refer to in their poetry, a theme echoed in the Song of Songs and by the great Spanish mystic St. John of the Cross.

We could see Jesus' crucifixion as the ultimate annihilation, the ultimate *'fanā*, but we could equally see his resurrection as the ultimate *baqā*, revivification. He survived the abject suffering of his body, his physical being. He survived also the stripping of all the layers of his psyche, everything he held dear, and anything he could have possibly held on to as a self-identity. He survived even the desolation of his spiritual being, his own sense of union with God, as he cried out " 'Eli, Eli lema sabachtani?' that is, 'My God, my God, why have you abandoned me?' "[63] And then he comes bounding back, as the Song of Songs says, "leaping upon the mountains, bounding over the hills"[64] on the third day. In our tradition we read the Song of Songs in the days after Easter just for this reason. It was a favorite of the medieval monastic writers such as the twelfth-century monk Bernard of Clairvaux, as well as the sixteenth-century Carmelites and their tradition of mystical marriage.

To our surprise, union with God and the so-called annihilation does not destroy our natural capacities, does not

63. Matt 27:46.
64. Song 2:8.

destroy our real self, *hidden with Christ in God,* but fulfills them! When the obscuring egoism has been stripped away, we discover the divine presence at the heart of our own being, and from this we experience greater self-realization and greater self-control. In this *baqā*-revival, we come bounding back from the '*fanā*-annihilation more fully human, the ideal human-ness that God intended all along.

Religion scholar Karen Armstrong too suggested that what Sufis are describing is the same state that the Greek Christians call "deification." Saint Bernard of Clairvaux, who was one of our great Western mystics and a Doctor of the Church, described the process in this beautiful poetic way:

> As a drop of water seems
> to disappear completely
> in a big quantity of wine,
> even assuming the wine's taste and color;
>
> just as red, molten iron
> becomes so much like fire
> it seems to lose its primary state;
>
> just as the air on a sunny day
> seems transformed into sunshine
> instead of being lit up;
>
> so it is necessary for the saints
> that all human feelings melt
> in a mysterious way
> and flow into the will of God.

Otherwise, how will *God be all in all* . . . ?[65]

Does something human survive in us?
No doubt, the substance remains
though under another form,
another glory, another power.[xxviii]

sister disciplines

In the past, and still today, we have thought of philosophy as the handmaiden of theology—*philosophia ancilla theologiae* is the ancient Latin maxim. Philosophy gives us a language to express revelation in a logical way rather than relying on iconographic and symbolic language, language that is generally more poetic than precise. This is why all priests at one time had to study four years of philosophy before embarking on four more years studying theology. Even to this day, though a full four years is not required in most seminaries, anyone entering seminary studies has to have a minimum requirement of philosophy or else spend some years in pre-theology studying enough philosophy to give the budding theologian the language and logic to frame theological arguments.

In a similar vein, just as the language of philosophy has helped us articulate theology, in modern times we have come to appreciate the language of psychology as a valuable

65. 1 Cor 15:28.

and indispensable language to articulate spirituality, much more than in the past. (In the big picture of history, psychology is a relatively new science.) Remember that the Greek word *psyche*—the root of psychology, psychotherapy, psychologist, and psychiatrist—is usually translated as "soul." So therapists at their best are really "soul doctors."

One of the reasons for the success and attraction of the Asian spiritual traditions is that they often have a much more practical and detailed map of the inscape of the mind and the soul than our Western Christian tradition has. Sometimes the mystical traditions of Asia are even referred to as the "psychological traditions," since more attention is paid to the dynamics of the inner life. While this is not unknown in the Christian contemplative tradition either, it has not been in our popular vocabulary as much as the language of devotion and adherence to principles is. This gap has been taken up in the West by psychology. As a matter of fact, the lament is often heard that psychology has all but replaced spirituality; even in some religious communities the "therapeutic model" has become the norm.

What is optimal is to see psychology and spirituality as sister disciplines. It works both ways: the best psychologists know that they can lead a patient or a client only so far, and then the spiritual traditions take over. In the same way, the best spiritual directors know that at times no more progress can be made in the spiritual life until the psychological blockages have been worked out, work that can only be done with someone trained in that specific area. The work of someone like the integral theorist Ken Wilber, for instance, has provided a useful new vocabulary that melds the wisdom of "the Traditions," as he calls them, with the insights of modern psychology, particularly in mapping out the stages and lines of growth as well as the evolution of consciousness—individual, cultural, and general—and showing how psychological growth and spiritual growth intersect and interact—and they do!

Jungian psychoanalysis and depth psychology in particular have a fascination for contemplatives. I've been heavily influenced by transpersonal psychology, particularly the work of Michael Washburn, who gave me a whole new vocabulary to explain the soul journey of the ascetical life. If I can do him justice, much of what follows here is drawn from his major work, *The Ego and the Dynamic Ground*. I hope by the end you will see how it ties into our discussion of kenosis.

the great mother

> The primary issue for the human family at its present level of evolutionary development is to become fully human. But that means discovering our connectedness to God, which was repressed somewhere in early childhood.[xxix]

There is a beautiful canticle from the prophet Isaiah, chapter 66, one of those rare places where we find a feminine image of God in the Bible: "As a mother comforts her child so will I comfort you . . ."[66] With all due respect and reverence for the inspired metaphor of God as Father, Jesus' *Abba*, imagine for a moment God as a mother. Not in the sense of another idol that we need to cast down from its throne, but as a womb from which we come forth.

This is perfectly orthodox Christianity. As article 239 of the *Catechism of the Catholic Church* explains it, "God's parental tenderness can also be expressed by the image of motherhood, which emphasizes God's immanence, the intimacy between Creator and creature." God as intimate as well as *immanent*, operating from within, pervading and sustaining, an active agent inside us—like yeast, like salt.

We human beings come into being—*ex nihilo*, from nothing, from "no-thing"—from God who is not just *like*, but really *is* the dynamic ground, the ground of all being and the ground of all consciousness. You might say that we come into being as if from a womb of possibility and potentiality, the divine womb as well as our mother's womb.

This is switching the image of our own origin in the same way as we have changed our image of God and Christ. Just as God is not Zeus sitting on top of Mount Olympus capriciously intervening, and Jesus is not a god leaping down fully formed from the same place, so too we are not souls that have been sent down from heaven to take up

66. Isa 66:13.

residence in a body. We come forth from God, who is the ground of being, as body and soul, or better, as an en-souled body or an incarnate soul, as if from that same womb of possibility and potentiality.

Recall this scene in the Gospel of John:

> There was a Pharisee named Nicodemus, a leader of the Jews. He came to Jesus by night and said to him, "Rabbi, we know that you are a teacher who has come from God; for no one can do these signs that you do apart from the presence of God." Jesus answered him, "Very truly, I tell you, no one can see the kingdom of God without being born from above." Nicodemus said to him, "How can anyone be born after having grown old? Can one enter a second time into the mother's womb and be born?" Jesus answered, "Very truly, I tell you, no one can enter the kingdom of God without being born of water and Spirit. What is born of the flesh is flesh, and what is born of the Spirit is spirit."[67]

Our evangelical brothers and sisters have made being "born again" central to their spirituality and message, and I certainly agree that it is necessary at some point in our life. But what does it really mean to be "born again"? I have an understanding of it that may differ from the usual sense.

67. John 3:1-6.

If we can know anything about prenatal consciousness, we could speculate that our first experience of being and life is *ouroboric*, an odd term meaning all-inclusive, with no clear sense of a distinction between our own selves and the dynamic ground from which we come, no clear sense of the difference between ourselves and our mother's womb and, what's equally important, not even a clear sense of the difference between the dynamic ground (the Divine) and our mother's womb. And our first experience of life as a newborn child is not that much different as we "nurse with delight at mother's consoling breast," to use Isaiah's imagery.

So we might say—and remember this is all poetry trying to describe the indescribable—that our first experience of the Divine is actually archetypally feminine, more maternal than paternal, because our birth mother is our first icon of Absolute Reality and the Divine. Washburn, following other Jungians and the Chinese mystical text the *Tao Te Ching*, refers to this experience as "the Great Mother."

In contradiction to others in his field, Washburn believes that there is already at least a seed of *ego* (and I mean "ego" here with nothing negative about it), already an incipient sense of an "I" in the womb. And transpersonal psychology suggests that our trajectory from birth on is toward becoming and fully realizing that "I" as an autonomous generative person who has come bursting forth—from God, we theists would say—with creative energy. My confrere Bruno Barnhart, in his seminal work, *The Future of Wisdom*, suggested that this is the foundational gift of

Western Christian thought as opposed to Asian thought, because it is Western Christianity that gave birth to the idea of the autonomous person, a separate self with individual rights. But in order to achieve and fulfill that autonomy and generativity there is a necessary movement away from the embedment and enmeshment in the mother. We all have to cut the apron strings at some point.

Washburn suggests that it is at this stage of development that we "discover," you might say, the father. He re-interprets what Freud called the Oedipal complex by suggesting that in what, until recent times, has been the normative family unit, the "father" is experienced as not only the first "other," but as an other who is both intimate and independent. The father can go off to work and yet still enjoy the affection of the mother. And so the child starts to imitate this, perhaps in the "terrible twos," learning how slowly, slowly, to wean itself from the enmeshment in mother's body and affection, and attempting to find the right balance between intimacy and independence. We can take any value judgment from this; it is not good or bad, sin or virtue. It is simply the natural trajectory of growth toward the establishment of an autonomous, generative self.

(Side note: I wonder if this couldn't serve also as a metaphor for human consciousness in general, in the broadest evolutionary sweep possible, that what goes on in every child is also what humanity went through in its own evolution of consciousness. In other words, did we as a human race at some point in our own evolution of consciousness start to image and relate to God as a father—outside of us? Some scholars of religion think so, that this occurred around the last centuries before the Common Era, the beginning of the so-called Axial Age.)

Unfortunately, as we break away from our birth mother we also break away from the Great Mother from whom we have come forth, the dynamic ground of being and ground of consciousness. Up until this point—again, as much as we can really know about the consciousness of even a newborn child—Washburn suggests that we still have a sense of unity with the natural world and are polymorphously sensual in our own bodies (meaning that our erotic sensibility has not yet constellated or trapped itself in specific erogenous zones); and up until this point we still experience the spiritual as dynamic, without a real split between the body and the spirit, because we are still in communion with our own mother and the dynamic ground. Up to this point we still experience the dynamic power of the ground as *our own power* as well.

But now, we slowly start to leave behind both our body and our spirit, and become solely a "mental ego" instead. In other words, we climb into our heads! We become more and more like a little person controlling our bodies as if riding around like a machine operator. Folks will even start to think that they "have" a body, not that they *are* their body. And the dynamism of the spiritual dimension gets lost almost completely. We're all "in our heads."

And so we have the famous phrase of the seventeenth-century French philosopher René Descartes, *Cogito ergo sum*—"I think therefore I am." The philosopher Richard Tarnas describes this as "the epochal defining statement of the modern self,"[xxx] making Descartes the father of modern Western culture, even of modern world culture. Now the thinking, rational self is seen as being separate from the rest of the universe, not only cut off from the dynamic ground of the spiritual realm, not only cut off from our own bodiliness and embeddedness in nature, but also cut off from real immersion in social life and the collective. We feel ourselves to be self-contained impermeable units without a real sense of our relation to, even unity with, other independent units, other people and the natural world.

Moving again from the micro to the macro, this is one of the things that the best minds of our generation are trying to address and redress with our budding global and ecological consciousness.

the sacrifice of our autonomy

> I may not be able to see it right now,
> but the Holy One fills all creation;
> being, itself, is made of God;
> you and I—everything is made of God.
> Even the grains of sand beneath my feet,
> the whole world is included and, therefore,
> utterly dissolved within God—
> while I, in my stubborn insistence
> on my own autonomy and independence,

only succeed in banishing myself
from any possibility of meaning whatsoever.

Kalynomous Kalmish Shapira
of Piesetzna[xxxi]

But there's hope. Not only *can* we, but Washburn suggests that in order to fulfill our humanness to the highest degree it is at this point that we *must*: we can and must recover the dynamic power of the ground. We have to go back to the Great Mother.

The problem is that this return to the Mother, the return to the dynamic ground, will be experienced as a kind of death, and perhaps you will see here where our notion of kenosis starts to enter the picture. This return to the "womb" feels at first like a sacrifice of our autonomy, our independence, our whole way of being in the world. But this is exactly the sacrifice, the death, that we have to undergo in the spiritual life—the sacrifice of our autonomy. Recall again the words of Psalm 40, which the author of the Letter to the Hebrews puts on the lips of the Christ:

Sacrifice and offering you do not desire,
    but you have given me an open ear.
Burnt offering and sin offering
    you have not required.
Then I said, "Here I am . . ."[68]

68. Ps 40:6-7; cf. Heb 10:5-7.

This is where the specifically Christian vocabulary and the icon of Christ are as eloquent as, and perhaps more so than, any other tradition, because this is the kenosis of Christ and the self-emptying of Jesus: Jesus' descent into the tomb becomes a return to the womb of new birth. This is also what the baptismal experience is supposed to be all about: a death and a re-birth. The good news is that what feels like death—sacrificing our autonomy—is not the end. It's the beginning of new life in Christ.

In the mystical language of ancient Greece, which the early Christian mystical writers adopted almost immediately, this experience was referred to as a "return to the One," and it seems to end there. In the Asian traditions of Hinduism, Buddhism, and Taoism, when we make this return to our origin the sense of distinct identity disappears back into the Great Mother "like a drop into the ocean," and it seems to end there. But our Christian image of the resurrection tells us instead that this isn't the end. It's just the beginning! It is at this point that the human person awakens once again to our union with the divine as our own identity: "it is no longer I who live, but it is Christ who lives in me."[69] That re-awakening leads me to experience the divine power within myself as my own generative freedom and "the capability of creating a human world."[xxxii]

69. Gal 2:20.

As the Sufis teach, the *'fanā*-annihilation is followed by *baqā*-revival, a re-vivification, a return to the self, but a return to an enhanced self. Kenosis has led not just to the cross and resurrection, but to Pentecost, which is the love of God poured into our hearts by the Spirit living in us.[70] Then comes new creation, a phrase that Paul uses twice, in the Letter to the Corinthians: "So if anyone is in Christ, there is a new creation: everything old has passed away; see, everything has become new"; and again in Galatians: "For neither circumcision nor uncircumcision is anything; but a new creation is everything!"[71]

Think for a moment of Baptism and Eucharist as the two fundamental Christian sacraments, with two complementary energies. The realization of our union with God is our *baptismal* energy, when we hear the voice over our heads, as Jesus did, "This is my beloved," and we know and have a sense that the love of God has been poured into our hearts by the Spirit living in us. That knowledge of our identity, those baptismal waters, then, become in us a river of life-giving water. "As the scripture has said, 'Out of the believer's heart shall flow rivers of living water.' "[72] This is spiritual dynamism, the source of our going out of ourselves in communion and participation. This is also the *eucharistic* energy, the energy of communion with others and nature

70. Rom 5:5.
71. 2 Cor 5:17; Gal 6:15.
72. John 7:38.

as well as with God in Christ. And we recover what we didn't even realize we had lost: the dynamism of the spiritual—and of the Spirit—as well as our sense of a unitive relationship with the natural world.

Here, by the way, is why it is called "transpersonal" psychology. In this process the self doesn't actually disappear like a drop into the ocean, but instead comes bursting forth from this death to move forward again with spiritual dynamism, a relationship with the body and the earth recovered. We evolve now *beyond* person—not pre-personal but *trans*-personal, to communion with others, with nature, with God. This is not just our own dynamic ground: this is the dynamic ground of *everything* because it is Being itself. And as we know, from St. Thomas Aquinas all the way up to the great Lutheran theologian Paul Tillich, God is not *a* being: God is Being itself, *esse ipsum*. So along with *us* being a new creation, the prophet Isaiah, Peter in his epistle, and John at the very end of the Book of Revelation all dream of "new heavens and a new earth,"[73] all that shares Being. To paraphrase Paul, again from the Letter to the Romans, all creation is groaning and in agony while we work this out, this redemption of our bodies. The new creation begins with the human person and catalyzes a rebirth of all creation. This is the priesthood of the human person.

---

73. Isa 65:17, 66:22; 2 Pet 3:13; Rev 21:1.

This is also the Christian mystical vision at its most refined.

This all sounds terribly arcane and complex, but let's boil it down to this simple truth: we need to re-establish our link with the immanent, intimate dynamic ground of being and consciousness, which is our own dynamic ground—and who is God—if we want to be fully human and grow into the likeness of God, both as individual human beings and as a race. This is our priesthood, and it will demand a kind of death for us, a kenosis, a sacrifice of our autonomy, a sacrifice perhaps of the ways of thinking and the lifestyles to which we have grown accustomed. But out of the ashes of our normal way of thinking and our accustomed way of being in the world (which I must say is not going very well for us as a race right now) can arise and will arise the phoenix of a new consciousness, a new way of being in the world, a new way of living gently on the planet, as well as a new way of understanding our communion with each other across peoples, languages, and ways of life, a participatory consciousness, participating, as St. Peter says, in the divine nature itself,[74] and participating as co-creators in a new earth.

74. 2 Pet 1:4.

But first, as the Jungian psychoanalyst James Hillman wrote, "at this moment of transition we cannot advance until we have first retreated enough inward and backward so that the unconscious . . . within us can catch up with us."[xxxiii]

This too is our kenosis, the movement inward and backward.

looking to heaven, looking within

Now, finally, we can speak about prayer and meditation.

Luke recounts an interesting parable that is about both prayer and the danger of being too smug. He lets us know that Jesus addresses this example specifically to those "who trusted in themselves that they were righteous and regarded others with contempt."

"Two men went up to the temple to pray, one a Pharisee and the other a tax collector." Remember that Pharisees were known for their piety and their scrupulous observance of the laws and practices of their faith, whereas tax collectors were practically considered outcasts, suspected both of being in cahoots with the Roman oppressors and of skimming money off the top for their own profit.

> The Pharisee, standing by himself, was praying thus,
> "God, I thank you that I am not like other people:
> thieves, rogues, adulterers, or even like this tax collector. I fast twice a week; I give a tenth of all my
> income." But the tax collector, standing far off,

would not even look up to heaven, but was beating his breast and saying, "God, be merciful to me, a sinner!"

Jesus says that it is this man, the outcast tax collector and not the pious righteous Pharisee, who went down to his home justified rather than the other: "for all who exalt themselves will be humbled, but all who humble themselves will be exalted."[75] This last phrase goes along with "those who find their life will lose it, and those who lose their life for my sake will find it"[76] as among the great paradoxes of the gospel teaching that are perennially difficult to understand, particularly perhaps by those who have been wounded by abuse and schooled in the language of recovery and emotional intelligence. But it is essential for our understanding of the radical kenosis the spiritual life calls for.

Focus for a moment just on the postures of these two characters. Luke makes a point to tell us that the Pharisee was standing by himself, alone, independent, self-contained and self-assured (autonomous!)—and he is looking up to heaven. The tax collector, on the other hand, does not even dare look up. We might hazard to say, however, that the tax collector is looking *within*, since he is acknowledging his failings in that moment, doing a kind of examination of conscience. The New American Bible may not be the most

75. Luke 18:9-15.
76. Matt 10:39.

accurate translation of this passage, but it has very acute, ironic, and humorous poetry to it. It says that the Pharisee prayed "to *himself*." He is looking up to heaven, but he is really talking to himself, admiring his reflection in a mirror, and projecting onto God his own image of righteousness and holiness. The tax collector, on the other hand, is looking at himself by looking within, but he really is praying to God.

sin and conversion

One of the things that Christianity gets criticized for often is its overemphasis on sin, all the way from ministers preaching about hellfire and brimstone to people teasing well into their adult years about recovering from "Catholic guilt." Certainly if that is the main message or the only message that remains, then there is something way off. But Jesus teaches in this parable that there is a truth in that message of repentance. Very often what people experience in the first throes of a conversion is a sense of all that they have gotten wrong up to that point. Often people turn to religion or spirituality because they are unhappy, unsettled, or unsatisfied with their life as it is, and having caught a glimpse of a possibility of joy, health, or peace, they are willing to undertake radical steps to access that same joy, health, or peace. When I was in college we could always tell when one of our friends had fallen in love because he would suddenly clean up his room, start to exercise and lose weight, maybe act a little less like a barbarian, wanting to present his best self to the beloved. This is actually an image of repentance and asceticism at its best, for a totally positive purpose.

Often, I will simply change the language if the word "sin" is too loaded with extra baggage, and speak instead about health versus addiction (back to St. Paul—we do not do what we want but what we hate); or else I speak about dysfunction, the ways of being in the world that we innocently inherit from our family systems and cultural upbringing. This is not to let us off the hook, turn us into victims, or release us from responsibility, but to put it all in a context of greater understanding. This is another area where psychological therapy as well as recovery programs can be enormously helpful.

Even more important, I never want to begin a conversation with "Look at what a sinner you are." I want to begin the conversation with "Look at how beautiful you are! Your inner self agrees with the law of God! Look at how fearfully, wonderfully, you have been made: you are created in the image of God and can move to being like God! Look at what dignity you are endowed with, the possibility and the hope of participating in divinity!" Now the focus becomes not so much on acknowledging our sinfulness but rather on living up to our beauty, marvel, and dignity, and ridding ourselves of all that is not godly.

This is a first and necessary kenosis. In the classic language of the spiritual life it's called the purgative way, and it is a very necessary initial phase. The problem occurs when we get stuck there. Now it's time to move on and forward into deeper relationship with God—and with our own selves. Now is a time to keep looking within and not only "up" to heaven, a deeper and subtler glance in search of what has been promised by Scripture: the love of God that is poured into our hearts by the Spirit living *in us* and the stream of life-giving water that Jesus said would flow out of the believer's heart, our real selves hidden with Christ in God, which lie buried under layers of unconscious and subconscious matter.

Now a whole new phase of the spiritual life opens up, as well as a new moment of prayer. This is when we begin the interior journey in earnest, the contemplative way. And it calls for a radical kenosis, an emptying out of whatever is blocking the stream of life-giving water from flowing out of my heart, ridding myself of whatever is standing between the image of God that is imprinted on the deepest part of my being and the face I actually present to the world. I am gazing within, like the tax collector, but not to focus on myself, let alone on my sins. I am now turning my gaze within to catch a glimpse of God, who is the source of my being.

Bede Griffiths, writing about his own conversion experience in his autobiography *The Golden String*, described it like this:

> there is an inner sanctuary into which we scarcely ever enter. It is the ground or substance of the soul, where all the faculties have their roots, and which

is the very centre of our being. It is here that the
soul is at all times in direct contact with God.[xxxiv]

To use the Advent language of Isaiah and John the Baptist,
in order to access that inner sanctuary where we are in
direct contact with God we need to prepare a highway in
the wilderness of our hearts. This is why Thomas Keating
could write about "unloading the unconscious," and taught
that prayer is not so much about experiencing peace as it
is evacuating "the unconscious obstacles to the abiding state
of union with God." So we are not just looking for contemplative prayer; we are hoping for a contemplative state. We
are not looking for "experiences, however exotic or reas-
suring, but the permanent and abiding awareness of God
that comes through the restructuring of consciousness,"[xxxv]
a re-structuring that only happens when we unload the
unconscious of all that is not godly, all that is not natural
to us who have been created in the image of God, of all that
does not agree with the law of God written on our hearts.

the milk of consolation

Let's go back to Isaiah's "Canticle of the Mother" again:

> That you may nurse and be satisfied
> from her consoling breast;
> that you may drink deeply with delight
> from her glorious bosom. . . .

You shall nurse and be carried on her arm,
and dandled on her knees.
As a mother comforts her child,
so I will comfort you.[77]

One of the advantages of psychology over philosophy is that psychology often takes symbolic and mythical language seriously, the language of universal archetypes and even the symbolism of dreams, trying to decipher the hidden meanings that float to the surface from deep in our unconscious minds in moments of sleep and surrender. Symbolic and mythical language is very close to the language of Scripture. To speak of something as a "myth," for example, is not to say that it is not true. It is only to say that it is trying to convey truth in a different way. This is not the language of history or science so much as it is the language of the inner world, the language of poetry and fables.

Returning to the maternal image of the Divine and Isaiah's canticle: perhaps it is not so much a prenatal return to the womb that we are in need of, but a return to the state of the newborn suckling at the breast as Isaiah invites us to. From a purely psychological point of view, James Hillman says that what is as important as the image of the "consoling breast" is the symbol of the milk that comes from that breast. And for Hillman the milk is a symbol of *sapientia*, primordial wisdom. (Recall that Wisdom is always

77. Isa 66:11, 12-13.

personified as feminine in the Jewish Scriptures.) What we need to recover is the primordial wisdom we had at the beginning, which is the knowledge of our union with the dynamic ground of Being, both a spiritual and a physical dynamism, in order to escape being trapped solely in our self-sufficient mental ego.

But the first thing that's required is the thirsting and the longing, like the tax collector in Luke's parable. The call for mercy is really a call for help, a craving for the milk of consolation. As Hillman points out, "The perfect and the powerful in their thrones," like the self-righteous Pharisee, "have no need of milk, wisdom and song." And then he quotes Jung himself, saying "It is from need and distress that new forms of existence arise"—and we might add that it is from need and distress that *new creation* arises too. My soul "is opened by admitting my weakness and my need," as the tax collector did, "for these needs make me a human creature, dependent in my creatureliness upon the creation and the Creator. . . . And we cannot meet these needs ourselves, self-enclosed, tight-lipped."[xxxvi] The cry for mercy, then, becomes a recognition of my creatureliness, an acknowledgement of my rootedness in Being itself, a longing for a return, and a sacrifice of my autonomy.

As mentioned earlier, this return to the mother, the sacrifice of my autonomy, can seem like a dissolving, like a drop of water re-entering the ocean. But Hillman points out that the image of drinking the milk at the breast is one of imbibing nutrition, and not an image of dissolution. "I take the milk into my body rather than its taking my body into itself and dissolving me in the oceanic bliss of the mother." Nutrition is not merely regression. The "I" does not disappear; the "I" remains and is nourished. "The milk of wisdom enters me, my mouth, and runs over my tongue into my belly" and "I am changed from within, from the center outward."

And what is this primordial wisdom that the milk represents? What do we learn in this experience? What is this *sapientia*? It is "knowledge of ourselves as we are in essence, as we are upon entering the world and [as we are] leaving it," *fearfully, wonderfully made.* What we learn is our dependence, our need. Or, to put it positively, we realize our union, our connection, because in our essence our real self agrees with the way of heaven and earth, the creation and the Creator. It is when that union is broken and our connection with the ground of being is gone that we are less than human.[xxxvii]

There are so many classic one-line descriptions of prayer and meditation. Let me add my own humble offering. Prayer—and I mean by "prayer" contemplative prayer, meditation in the Christian understanding—prayer is like nursing at the breast of God, drinking the milk of holy Wisdom.

In the classic language of the spiritual life we have now moved from the purgative way to the illuminative way, the way of holy Wisdom.

new creation, new heavens, new earth

I find it instructive that the long Book of the Prophet Isaiah ends with this Canticle of the Mother and its message of comfort. It is also instructive that it is here, immediately after this passage, that Isaiah prophesies about "the new heavens and the new earth"[78] that God will bring about. There can be no new creation without a return to our connection with our source, our ground, the Holy One, the Great Mother. There can be no new creation unless and until we recover what we didn't even know we had lost. As another canticle, at the end of the Book of Deuteronomy, sings, "you were unmindful of the Rock that bore you; you forgot the God who gave you birth."[79] But the promise is that there will be a new creation when we return to the milk of holy Wisdom, when we re-establish our connection with our source, our ground, the God Who Gave Us Birth—and recover what we didn't even know we had lost.

Furthermore, there can be no new creation without the restructuring of our consciousness that comes about through this radical kenosis. This applies to the individual as well as to humanity in general. What Albert Einstein said many years ago applies even more now: the problems we face as a race are not going to be solved by the same consciousness that created the problems. I want to add, however, that the

78. Isa 66:22.
79. Deut 32:18.

new consciousness can only come about by the radical kenosis offered by the spiritual life, being "changed from within, from the center outward."

Here we return once again to the great kenosis hymn of Paul. Yes, we too can have the mind of Christ, "Christ consciousness," if you will. But all the modern spiritual masters that I have studied teach that this radical kenosis is the essential ingredient for the mind of Christ, Christ consciousness. The late Irish Benedictine John Main, speaking of the Christian understanding of contemplative prayer and meditation, explained it this way: Jesus' own prayer is "the stream of his consciousness fully open to the Father." And each one of us in turn is invited to "open our consciousness fully to the consciousness of Jesus," as Paul says, to "let the same mind be in you that was in Christ Jesus." In that openness we are "taken out of ourselves, beyond ourselves, into that stream of conscious love which flows between Jesus and the Father."xxxviii

Prayer—contemplation, meditation—then becomes a way of fulfilling the gospel mandate that "Those who find their life will lose it, and those who lose their life will find it,"[80] because in contemplative prayer you "lose your consciousness of yourself as an autonomously separate, separated entity." And in losing it, "you find yourself at one with God and at one with all creation because you are now at last

---

80. Matt 10:39.

one with yourself," your true self, hidden with Christ in God. In that experience of losing ourselves we are, paradoxically, "made completely and eternally real" and we know ourselves for the first time—because we are lost in God.[xxxix]

Pie Pelicane

The evocative pre-Christian image of the *Pie Pelicane*, the holy pelican, has long been my favorite christic and eucharistic image. As best we can tell it doesn't actually jibe with zoology, but according to legend if her chicks don't have enough to eat the mother pelican will rip her own breast open and feed the chicks with her own flesh and blood. Please note that this is a *self-inflicted* wound. It's easy to see why this is an image of Christ and the eucharistic sacrifice.

There is yet another use of the icon of the holy pelican, in the ancient tradition of alchemy. Alchemy has roots in ancient Egyptian iconography and the Greek magical tradition. It was an occupation of some medieval monks (for example, the fifteenth-century Swiss monk, physician, and theorist Paracelsus) and in modern times has been a fascination not only of depth psychologists, but also of even such an eminent theologian as Hans Urs von Balthasar as well. The basic pseudo-scientific premise of alchemy is that so-called base metals such as lead, tin, iron, copper, and mercury (represented by the chicks feeding on mother pelican's breast), if exposed to enough heat, will melt down and devolve into what is called *materia prima*, prime matter, and then those base metals can and will transmute into precious metals, especially gold.

Alchemy, however, from the beginning was actually understood more as a metaphysical teaching than a hard science, symbolic of the journey of the soul—hence the fascination of the medieval monks and von Balthasar, as well as psychologists such as Carl Jung, who wrote extensively on it, and the aforementioned Michael Washburn. In fact Washburn says that Christianity and alchemy, along with the tantric yoga tradition of India, are three of the more important historical conceptions of regeneration in spirit.[xl] This is the same regeneration we have spoken of—being "born again"—that happens after we die to our autonomy in our return to God, the dynamic ground of being.

According to alchemy's use of the image of the pelican, the chicks, instead of representing base metals, now represent one's own psychic powers or soul forces, and the pelican is a symbol of the *materia prima*. But now the prime matter is understood to be Divine Love, the soul's forces returning to their source in Divine Love, which nurtures and nourishes them. At some point, instead of or in addition to being a symbol of a sacrificial relationship with and for others, like the real mother pelican, we enter into a sacrificial relationship with our own self, with our own inner being, and begin to sacrifice the inner powers of our own souls to the immanent and intimate love of God that is at the very center of our being. Thus we nourish the developing spiritual embryo, the new creation, within us. My image of myself—my persona, my false self—must be changed, transmuted, and sacrificed to the developing spiritual self that is *hidden with Christ in God*. This is normally a painful experience, akin to St. John of the Cross's dark night of the soul, that will take all my inner resources. It will feel like a death, a dissolving, like a caterpillar in its chrysalis that devolves into nothing but an amorphous glob before emerging as a butterfly. Just so, out of this dark night of the soul will emerge the spiritual self, transformed through the pelican experience. *I wish to dissolve and be with Christ.*

inscendence

The late Thomas Berry, the Passionist priest and geologian (as he referred to himself), thought that we, as a human race, had done enough with our *transcendence*, and have actually done damage to God's great gift of earth, as well as to our own humanity, by the neglect of those same things that our desire to transcend has inspired. Instead he taught that before we could evolve we needed to experience what he coined as *inscendence*. Whereas transcendence is our drive *away* from the world, *away* from creation, *away* from our bodies, inscendence is the movement within, the inward movement that is needed to complement and sometimes correct our transcendence. To disintegrate all the way down to the genius embedded in our DNA and start all over again, to descend to our instinctive resources in order to be re-invented. The bigger issue that Berry was addressing, of course, was not just individuals, but that as peoples, as nations, maybe as human civilization in general and our species collectively, from the micro to the macro, we must do so as well.[xli]

This is what has to happen at some point in everyone's spiritual journey, like our going back to the Mother: to reinvent ourselves by going down. This is also a good description of what we are being asked to do each year during the penitential season of Lent, the forty days in the desert, stripping down to basics, just as in the ascetical life in general. It is a sinking back into the source of everything, like Jesus in the desert, like Jesus in the tomb, those times when we "trust our unknowing and during which we no longer belong to the world in our old ways, a stranger again."[xlii] And there in the presence of the source of everything, we hope to be remade, reinvented, born again.

The physicality of all this in Thomas Berry's writing is important and not just meant as a metaphor. It's a firm belief that encoded in our DNA is the soul's code, the law written on our hearts, if you will, and the spiritual power that has been the thrust behind our evolution, in consciousness and otherwise, all along, the dynamic ground of our being and consciousness. Our *genetic* coding, that is, as opposed to our *cultural* coding: even our cultural coding must be stripped away too at some point, maybe especially, because here "there is no longer Jew or Greek, there is no

longer slave or free, there is no longer male and female."[81]
If we are reinvented, it is to make us what we have been or
have been meant to be all along that perhaps got covered
over by our cultural coding. But we must sacrifice our autonomy in order to rediscover it.

The late spiritual writer William Johnston wrote about
something similar to this in describing the mysticism of
The Cloud of Unknowing. This is the beauty of the practice
of contemplative prayer, of meditation and yoga, that we
do sink into our own bodily-ness to discover that which is
deeper than—and the source of—material reality, the
ground of our being and the ground of all consciousness.
And in this purified tranquility of darkness, as the *Cloud*
would call it, "the soul goes down, down to the very center
of its own being, nakedly to encounter God who secretly
dwells in silent love at the sovereign point of the spirit."[xliii]
That silent love is the *materia prima.*

devolve to evolve

We need to evolve in our understanding of who and what
God is, grow out of our mythical magical mindset, and
even beyond our rationality, finally discover the *Abba* of
Jesus, the God of the gospels, and build a new spirituality
and spiritual practice based on that knowledge of God—

81. Gal 3:28.

theo-logy, Christology, and *anthropo*-logy, knowledge of who we are as human beings. This is an urgent work: all of creation is groaning and in agony while we, the priests of creation, work this out.[82] But in order to evolve, something is going to have to die—our old ways of being in and understanding the world, and Ultimate Reality. We will first of all need to *devolve*.

It's important to note that the interior way and the exterior way, just as the contemplative life and the active life, are not mutually exclusive nor antagonistic, just as breathing in and breathing out are both necessary. The *Pie Pelicane* feeding its young from its very flesh is a eucharistic image not referring only to Christ, nor only to the sacred species that we receive and consume. It is a eucharistic image that we are meant not only to adore, but to imitate as well, as individuals, as a community, as a church. As Pope St. Leo the Great prayed, "Change us into what we receive!" We as individuals, whose lives have been held up like the bread and wine, blessed and sanctified, transubstantiated, are now called to be broken, like the fractioning of the bread, and passed out, crushed like grapes into holy wine and poured out in love and service, emptied and become servant footwashers.

All that we have said about God-as-Mother and the *Pie Pelicane* should also apply to Holy Mother Church. We as church also, collectively, are meant to give of our very es-

82. Cf. Rom 8:22-23.

sence for the sake of others in imitation of our Lord, even if we have to wound ourselves like Mother Pelican does in the process. We as a community, as a church, are meant to become Eucharist. As a twentieth-century hymn goes:

> Then let the servant church arise,
> A caring church that longs to be
> A partner in Christ's sacrifice,
> And clothed in Christ's humanity.[xliv]

This hearkens back to Hans Urs von Balthasar's dream of a "disinterested church," a church that doesn't seek its own glory, but the glory of its Lord and union as love. To be like a seed that falls into the ground and dies, to be like yeast in the dough, to act by dissolving and disappearing, like a mother pelican who is willing to rip her own breast open to feed her young. Willing even to wound herself to feed her young, to disappear, to dissolve, so as to nourish and flavor all that in which we are planted. Or as the beautiful Metta prayer of the Buddhist tradition has it, "Even as a mother protects with her life her only child, so with a boundless heart should we cherish all living beings." Would that Holy Mother Church would always have this heart and mind first and foremost.

Where do we find the strength to do this, to be this? From a return to our source, the sacrificial relation with our inner self and a return to the dynamic ground of our being and consciousness, *the God who gave us birth.*

One last image from Father Romuald. He ends his Brief Rule with two images of God, one very masculine and one very feminine and maternal. First of all, he says we should "stand before God with the attitude of one who stands before the emperor," a very masculine image from one who actually knew the emperor well. But then he ends by telling us that after we empty ourselves completely, we should "sit waiting . . . like a chick who tastes nothing and eats nothing but what its mother gives it."[xlv]

Let's empty ourselves, completely. And before we start to rebuild and reinvent ourselves, wait for our intimate and imminent God to feed us, to regenerate our soul's forces, and to make of us a new creation and of our earth a new earth, not in the image of our own creation again, but in the image of God who is Jesus our Lord.

Notes

i. Quoted in Paul Elie, *The Life You Save May Be Your Own* (New York: Farrar, Straus and Giroux, 2003), 424, 106.

ii. Nathan Mitchell, *Real Presence* (Chicago: Liturgy Training Publications, 1998), 47–48.

iii. Hans Urs von Balthasar, "Chi è il cristiano," author's translation, from Bose *Letture dei Giorni* (Casale Monferrato: Edizioni Piemme, 1994), 121–23.

iv. The Office of Readings (Boston: St. Paul Editions, 1983), 1579.

v. Raimundo Panikkar, *Il Silenzio del Buddha*, author's translation (Milano: Oscar Mondadori, 2006), 169.

vi. Christian Wiman, "Kill the Creature," *The American Scholar*, Spring 2015, https://theamericanscholar.org/kill-the-creature/.

vii. Joseph Ratzinger (Pope Benedict XVI), *Jesus of Nazareth: From the Baptism in the Jordan to the Transfiguration* (New York: Doubleday, 2007), 95.

viii. Tom Conry, "Anthem" (Portland, OR: Oregon Catholic Press, 1978).

ix. Quoted in Olivier Clement, *The Roots of Christian Mysticism* (New York: New City Press, 1995), 90.

x. Clement, *Roots of Christian Mysticism*, 90.

xi. Ingri and Edgar Parin d'Aulaire, *D'Aulaires' Book of Greek Myths* (New York: Doubleday, 1962), 70–72.

xii. Von Balthasar, "Chi è il cristiano," author's translation, 121–23.

xiii. This essay opens the first of two tomes of volume 7 of the *Opera Omnia* that gathers the writings on Vatican II published by the Vatican's *Libreria Editrice*, anticipated by the "Vatican Insider" feature of the Italian paper *La Stampa*, May 29, 2016.

xiv. Quoted in *Life You Save*, 368.

xv. *Benedictine Daily Prayer*, ed. Maxwell E. Johnson (Collegeville, MN: Liturgical Press, 2005), 727.

xvi. See Ryan Lizza's excellent article, "Leap of Faith," *The New Yorker*, August 15 and 22, 2011.

xvii. Al-Majilisi, *Bihar al-Anwar*, vol. 19, p. 182, hadith no. 31.

xviii. Pope Benedict XVI, *Spe Salvi* 15, http://www.vatican.va /content/benedict-xvi/en/encyclicals/documents/hf_ben-xvi _enc_20071130_spe-salvi.html.

xix. Benedict Groeschel, *Spiritual Passages* (New York: Crossroad, 1987), 143.

xx. *Meister Eckhart: The Man from Whom God Hid Nothing*, ed. Ursula Fleming (Springfield: Templegate Publishers, 1990), 49.

xxi. Thomas Merton, *Raids on the Unspeakable* (New York: New Directions, 1964), 88.

xxii. Merton quoted in *Life You Save*, 301.

xxiii. *Rumi's Little Book of Love*, trans. Maryam Mafi and Azima Melita Kolin (London: Thorsons Publishers, 2000), 208.

xxiv. Bruno di Querfurt, *Vita dei Cinque Fratelli* (*VF*), Italian trans. Bernardo Ignesti (Camaldoli: Edizioni Camaldoli, 1951), Cap. IV, 41, (Latin)115; English translations: Thomas Matus, *The Mystery of Romuald and the Five Brothers: Stories from the Benedictines and Camaldolese* (Trabuco Canyon: Source Books, 1994), 95; Peter Damian Belisle, trans., *Camaldolese Spirituality: Essential Sources* (Bloomingdale: Ercam Editions, 2007), 46.

xxv. *VF*, Cap. XIX, 92, (Latin)151; Matus, 158; Belisle, 102.

xxvi. *Essential Sufi*, ed. James Fadiman and Robert Frager (New York: HarperOne, 1997), 115.

xxvii. A. J. Arberry, *Sufism: An Account of the Mystics of Islam* (London: George Allen and Unwin, 1950), 58–59.

xxviii. *On Loving God* X:28, trans. Robert Walton (Collegeville, MN: Cistercian Publications, 1995); emphasis added.

xxix. Thomas Keating, *Invitation to Love*, in *Foundations for Centering Prayer and the Christian Contemplative Life* (New York: Continuum, 2006), 164.

xxx. Richard Tarnas, *The Passion of the Western Mind* (New York: Harmony Books, 1991), 275. See also Carter Phipps, *Evolutionaries* (New York: Harper, 2012), 158.

xxxi. *B'nei Makhsahva Tova*, p. 33, #14 (Hebrew) Jerusalem, 1989; trans. Lawrence Kushner, used with permission.

xxxii. Bruno Barnhart, *The Future of Wisdom* (New York: Continuum, 2007), 143.

xxxiii. *Puer Papers*, ed. James Hillman (Washington, DC: Spring Publications, 1979), 38.

xxxiv. Bede Griffiths, *The Golden String* (Springfield: Templegate, [1954] 1980), 104.

xxxv. Keating, *Open Mind, Open Heart*, in *Foundations for Centering Prayer*, 86.

xxxvi. *Puer Papers*, 39–40.

xxxvii. *Puer Papers*, 40–41.

xxxviii. *The Way of Unknowing*, quoted in *Stillness and Silence in Every Season*, ed. Paul Harris (New York: Continuum, 2002), 337.

xxxix. *Way of Unknowing*, in *Stillness and Silence*, 337.

xl. Michael Washburn, *The Ego and the Dynamic Ground* (New York: SUNY Press, 1995), 205.

xli. *Thomas Berry, Dreamer of the Earth*, ed. Ervin Laszlo and Allan Combs (San Francisco: Sierra Club Books, 1988), 42–69.

xlii. *Thomas Berry*, 50.

xliii. William Johnston, *The Mysticism of the Cloud of Unknowing* (Saint Meinrad: Abbey Press, 1975), 186.

xliv. Fred Pratt Green, "The Church of Christ in Every Age" (Carol Stream, IL: Hope Publishing Company, 1971).

xlv. *VF*, Cap. XIX, 92; Matus, 158; Belisle, 102.